CW00428237

BRIDE

The church that Jesus died for
and is coming back for

Endorsements

When some aspect of the church hurts us, we either walk away disappointed, stay and grow a bit cynical, or try to bring about change. But we cannot change the church of Jesus Christ until we love her as his bride. My friend Nic has spent his adult life loving, serving and beautifying the Bride of Christ faithfully, in his own city of Liverpool and around the world. This book is a kind of love-song to that Bride. Whether you're new to faith and trying to get your head around this thing called church, or a seasoned leader looking for renewed vision, Nic's message will inspire you with a fresh passion for who she can be, and a militant determination to conspire night-and-day for all that is to come!

Pete Greig, Emmaus Rd Church and 24-7 Prayer International.

Boring or annoying – that's how I often find books on the Church. I have numerous: weighty ecclesiological tomes by scholars; new methodologies from trendy post-Christendom post-moderns; books by abstract theoreticians who've never led worship, taught a sermon series, put out the chairs on Sunday or sat with the broken. Books from cultural revolutionaries and iconoclasts, books from the traditionalists or restorationists.
Nic Harding's Bride is different. Intelligent but accessible, Biblical and practical, visionary but rooted in 4 decades of pastoral experience – real yet hopeful. This is a brilliant handbook on Church. After 4 decades of faithful and fruitful leadership, through the good and the bad, in 'Bride' Nic Harding offers us a Biblical vision of the Church how she should be, and practical steps of how she can be that. I loved reading this book – it was balm to this tired pastor's soul. This should be read by newcomers to Church and those who've been in leadership for years. A real gem.

Simon Ponsonby, Pastor of Theology, St Aldates, Oxford

From The Ugly Duckling to Jane Eyre to present-day romances, literature is full of examples of characters, believing themselves to be broken or worthless, who are patiently loved into something glorious. My hope and prayer is that this wonderful book would achieve a similar transformation in the Church's mindset. There can be few more startling contrasts than that between how Jesus sees his Bride and how we see ourselves. Nic has done us a great favour by showing so clearly from scripture the role God's Bride is to play where she can finally reveal her true beauty.

Paul Harcourt, New Wine's National Leader and vicar at All Saints Woodford Wells

In The Screwtape Letters CS Lewis gave hell's game away with regard to the church. Enemy powers want us to focus on its faults and failings, remaining blind to its spiritual reality, "spread through all time and space and rooted in eternity, terrible as an army with banners." In this practical yet profound work Nic Harding lifts the veil on the beautiful bride of Christ so that we may fall in love again with her once more.

Anthony Delaney, Ivy Church Network, LAUNCH Church multiplication catalyst

In the church today there is a lot of talk about structure and strategy, often driven by results or fear of decline. Here Nic brings us back to our identity as the Bride of Christ and our intimate connection with him in the Spirit, and then draws out the practical implications of this and what it means to prepare for Christ's return. Full of great stories from Nic living this out in his own life, this book is food for your soul and fire to inspire you to live for Jesus Christ.

John McGinley, New Wine Director of Church Planting Development

This is a timely book calling the church towards her destiny and in doing that, calling us, as members of the church towards ours. It gets under your skin, as it paints a picture of church that many of us know it can be and which, deep down we know will truly please King Jesus, the bridegroom who is waiting for His bride. It is both visionary and equipping, giving many personal and inspiring examples from Nic's own life which provoke possibility thinking on how life can be lived more radically and more fruitfully. It is a rousing call to action and has come at just the right time when the re-set button has been pushed and churches are now navigating a new normal. This book helps us to re-imagine church in a way that is a truer reflection of its original purpose and design.

Ness Wilson, Pioneer UK Leader, Team Leader of Open Heaven Church

This is a valuable and helpful book. Faithful to his own tradition, Nic is at the same time a statesman in the Christian community, a bridge-builder and an elder brother for so many of us in the churches of the North-West. Growing disciples is at the heart of his life. His vision is compelling – to see a united, passionate, devoted community of people who are proud to be together as the bride of Christ. His book is biblically rich, practically useful, and filled with a desire to see the Church entering into her dignity as the chosen spouse of her Lord. It's an honour to commend it.

Paul Bayes, Anglican Bishop of Liverpool.

In 45 years of ministry, Nick has never lost the wonder of following Jesus. In "Bride", you will find lessons Nic has learnt that will inject hope, passion and fruitfulness into your Christian life. Buy it, read it, ponder the questions at the end of each chapter and put them into practice. Your life will never be the same.

David Stroud, Senior Leader, Christ Church and Leader/Co-Founder, Everything Conference

In his book 'Bride', Nic shares an important prophetic message for the Church today, as well as excellent teaching on how we can function as disciples together according to God's plan. If you are a Christian who is seeking to follow Jesus, this book will challenge and equip you to step into the fullness of what it is to be a part of His Church. Nic teaches from the Bible but also out of his own life, which will inspire you to step out more into the radical lifestyle to which Jesus calls us. I strongly recommend this book!

Paul Maconochie, 3DM team leader: USA and Canada.

In this powerful work, Nic Harding has brought together all aspects of being the church: the Head, the Heart and the Hands. We are not called to be a church of ill-consequence or pious passivity. Reading this book will make your heart leap, give your mind something to crunch, and an itchy sense in your feet that you should start getting to work. Best of all, there's a keen sense of situation within God's redemptive grace and ongoing work. I highly recommend it!

Doug Paul, Innovation Strategist with Catapult and Pastor of East End Fellowship, Richmond Virginia, USA

Nic's helpful and timely book seems to strangely mirror my own experience over the last 40 years. I too was inspired by the vision of church as recorded in the book of Acts and set off on an adventure of church planting and team ministry. Through the years, schism, broken relationships and anti-church viruses have sought to disempower and frustrate. This is a book I will highly recommend to pastors and leaders who need to continue to navigate the obstacles and pitfalls within our present culture pointing towards our future hope. I shall certainly be encouraging people to embrace the 'Bridal Charter' outlined in the last chapter.

Stuart Bell, Team leader of Ground Level Network and Senior Pastor of Alive Church, Lincoln

In an age of 'sophisticated' & often cynical discourse about the church, Nic offers an antidote. Here is an honest, confident, head-lifting vision for church life, from a real practitioner who unashamedly loves the bride.

Joel Virgo, Senior Pastor of Emmanuel, Brighton

A passionate vision from someone who loves the church for better and for worse. If you have fallen out of love with church, or have a jaded heart, Nic Harding has written a song of love for Jesus' bride which will reopen your eyes to her (and your own) potential beauty. It's also a clear, practical and accessible "marriage guidance" manual for being Church, and living into our calling – the accumulated and honest wisdom of a life of faithfulness to the Groom.

Guy Donegan-Cross, Director of Learning for Discipleship and Mission, Church of England, Birmingham.

I thank God for Nic and I'm glad he's written this engaging book! The book is an authentic description of the Christian understanding of the church, the Bride, bringing together practical, down to earth advice about heavenly-minded, missional living. Nic gives us a disciples' perspective and a leaders' handbook on real church in one piece of writing. He shares with us distilled wisdom from four decades' faithful following of Jesus and loving his church. I heartily recommend the book.

Aled Griffith, Leader Reach Nottingham and Team Leader Synergy Sphere

I have loved reading this book and now I want my whole church family to read it! As a follower of Christ and church leader, I found myself both challenged and encouraged, provoked and inspired. I found myself caught up with a fresh sense of passion for Christ and His bride and an increased desire to renew my commitment for serving Him and His beautiful church. I believe that would be true for every Christ follower, church member or leader. This is not just theory but practice; it is not just principles but real life examples, of both success and failure, from Nic's own life and ministry that reflect the journey of radical disciple trying to follow Jesus. May we each be envisioned again to give ourselves sacrificially and wholeheartedly to Christ and the church He gave Himself for.

Andy Barclay-Watt, Senior Leader of LifeChurch Manchester & Leader of the Maximise family of churches (part of Salt & Light)

Nic is a big-hearted and generous man who loves the church, not just his church, but God's church. This book will stir your passion for Jesus, the church and for mission. Nic has lived this out by serving the churches of Liverpool for 25 years, including the new churches that roll up. His passion is for believers to be living stones and not loose rubble, disciples on a mission for Jesus.

Graham Webb, Senior Pastor of Jubilee Church (New Frontiers), Liverpool

We loved this book. Like Nic's other books we finished it more hope-filled for the church. His combination of clear Scriptural thinking, real reproducible applications and the authenticity that comes from one who lives out the message he carries is both inspiring and empowering. Our hope is that many will hear a fresh call through these pages to live in their true identity as the Bride of Christ, and discover simple accessible ways to embrace this calling day by day.

Simon & Ceri Harris, Senior Ministers, Burlington Baptist Church, Ipswich

'Bride' – the word itself immediately conjures thoughts and emotions that lift our expectations. Words like, love, joy, celebrations, togetherness. But is this like the Church we know? As Nic's book shows there are other factors involved before we get there. Words like, 'the cost we have to pay', 'changes to be made', 'frustration and disappointments', but if we can keep our eyes fixed on the Wedding Day we can get there.

Phil Vogel, wise man and past mentor to Nic. Part of the Pioneer Network

Publishing details….

ISBN: 978-1-5272-1898-7
Date Published: July 24th, 2020

Scripture references in this book are from the following translations. The abbreviations are used, where needed, in some of the footnotes. Unless marked otherwise, the version will be the NIV

AMPC – Amplified Bible, Classic edition, published by the Lockman Foundation, 1965, 1987
ESV – English Standard Version, published by Crossway, 2001
J B Phillips translation of the New Testament, published by Archbishop's Council, 1960, 1972
NIV – New International Version, published by Biblica, 1978
NLT – New Living Translation, published by Tyndale House, 1996
NASB – The New American Standard Bible, published by the Lockman Foundation, 1960, 1971
TPT – The Passion Translation, published by Broadstreet Publishing Group, 2017.

Contents

Acknowledgements

I know it's conventional to refer to spouses and family when writing acknowledgements for a book. But I am quite sure that I am what I am today because of a marriage of 45 years to Jenny. I remember her as my bride all those years ago, when we committed ourselves to each other 'for better or for worse'. She has stood by me when I've made decisions she would probably have preferred me not to make. She trusted me in my decision to leave my medical career for the uncertain journey of church leadership. She followed me from Bristol to Liverpool when we planted Frontline Church. She has been my better half for all those years. She has enabled us to experience so much of what I talk about in this book, through her home-making, her hospitality, her parenting, and her wisdom, which has kept me out of trouble on many occasions. I think of her as my second Holy Spirit!

I want to also acknowledge my four wonderful daughters who have put up with our experiments in community living, and with the many women and men who have lived with us over the years. I know it hasn't always been easy.

I have a second Jennie that I also want to acknowledge. Jennie Taylor has been an amazing PA / Ops Manager / Co-leader within Kairos Connexion for the last 4 years. She has been so much more than I could have hoped when she first started. It's not often that you work with someone who just 'gets you'. It makes the working environment so much easier. She has complemented me brilliantly in all that the role of Kairos Connexion director has demanded. She has undoubtedly made all I have done with Kx possible, and she's definitely put the fun back into working life.

Thanks also to the many men and women, church leaders in Kairos Connexion and Together for the Harvest, who have trusted me in these last 5 years to lead and support them. I have learnt so much from you and treasured your friendship. Thank you.

Thanks so much to Sally Thomas, the Associate Vicar at St Paul's Howell Hill, who has faithfully given me editorial support through the writing of this book. Thanks to her and Neil for allowing me to use their cottage to write the first draft. It was a haven of undistracted bliss.

Dedication

This book is dedicated to those pilgrims of faith who have a sense that 'there must be more to church life than this!' Those who are willing to leave the safety of the harbour, the status quo, to explore the untamed oceans of possibility of what the church that Jesus died for and is coming back for could be like.

Foreword

What I'm about to say might sound a bit gushing, over-the-top, sycophantic even; but when Nic Harding says something, I listen. I pay attention because I have found that what he has to say is usually pure gold. Nic may not have the online profile and presence of some superstar preachers. He might not have the social media following or the skinny jeans and hipster haircut of a self-proclaimed leadership guru celebrity pastor, but when Nic asked me to read his book I made it a priority. Why? Because I knew it would challenge me in my discipleship journey and equip me to live the sort of Christian life that I long for.

And I have every reason to say this with confidence. Just over 20 years ago I was a young man with a fresh Bible College degree and a whole load of head knowledge. When it came to church, I thought I knew it all, had seen it all, and now I was about to show the world how it should be done. Then I met Nic and the fledgling Frontline Church community in Liverpool. A handful of people meeting in a semi-derelict Territorial Army Centre. And what I saw, what I heard, what I experienced blew my mind. Nic invited my wife and I to move to Liverpool and be apprenticed by him. So we did. And the rest is history, as they say.

So when I read 'Bride', I don't read it as theory or good suggestions. I read it as tried and tested principles that really work, principles that I've seen Nic live out and model over two decades. Principles that I've tried to imitate as I've been discipled by Nic. So for example, when Nic says discipleship happens around the meal table, let me tell you, he means it. There have been seasons in my life where it was almost like we had more meals around Nic and Jen's table than our own.

And we laughed. And cried. And squirmed at the challenge. And rejoiced in the breakthroughs. Through those days Nic became more than a mentor to me. Nic became a spiritual father. Nic is the real deal.

I hope as you read this book you too will capture from Nic a compelling vision for the beautiful Bride of Jesus, as I have, a vision worth giving your life for.

John Harding
Senior Pastor, Frontline Church Liverpool (and no relation!)

Who is this book for?

This book is for men and women who find themselves saying 'There must be more to church life than this'. For leaders and members who have got used to a way of being and doing church that no longer arouses wonder, awakens desire, or imparts hope. Frankly, they are bored with church.

It reminds me of the joke about the man who's mother comes into his bedroom on a Sunday morning telling him it's time to get up and get ready to go to church. After the man's protestations that he wants to stay in bed, and that he finds church boring, his mother in exasperation says 'Well you've got to go, you are the vicar!'

It's a book that is designed to inspire, to challenge, and to help reshape our ideas of what church could and maybe should be. It's an exploration of the church as shaped by Jesus' soon return. I hope it helps you get excited to be a vital part of the one thing that is most important to Jesus, the one thing that he has spent all of eternity dreaming of – his glorious Bride.

Introduction

L et us rejoice and be glad and give him glory!
For the wedding of the Lamb has come, and his bride has made herself ready.[1]

'I love Jesus, I just don't have time for the church'. It's a phrase often heard.
People seem to have either become disillusioned and disconnected from church, or are just too busy and pre-occupied with their own life. But can we love Jesus without loving his body?

A good friend of mine, Jimmy, says that if someone comes to his house to see him, and even though his wife and kids are in the room, doesn't show real appreciation for, or any interest in them, then that is probably the last time they will be invited over. How someone treats our spouse says a lot about what they really think of us. Perhaps they just wanted something from us, rather than having a genuine interest in us and our spouse or family. Maybe our relationship with them is just a transactional one.

The church is the Bride of Christ. And here's the thing: we cannot say we want to know Jesus, and then ignore his Bride, his family. We can't love Jesus and not love what he loves most, his beautiful Bride. This book is hopefully going to provide some ideas of what that Bride is intended to be like, and how our love for her can show honour to Jesus. After

---

[1] Rev 19:7 NIV

all, she is the one he died for and is coming back for, to spend all eternity with.

What would it look like for that great and final day to shape all that we did in the here and now?

So much of church leadership, church involvement, and church development is expedient, it is responding to immediate pressure, to the latest fashions of the day, and to what we as leaders think is expected of us. What would it look like for that great and final day to shape all that we did in the here and now? For church to be prepared as a Bride, in holy and breath–holding expectation of that day?

This book is a simple vision for that church, and an invitation to become the Bride.

The Why?

In the closing chapters of the Bible we read this about the church, the Bride.

Let us rejoice and be glad and give the glory to Him, for the marriage of the Lamb has come and His bride has made herself ready.[1]

And I saw the holy city, new Jerusalem, coming down out of heaven from God, made ready as a bride adorned for her husband.[2]

However you interpret the images and metaphors of the book of Revelation, there is no mistaking that the church is central to all of God's purposes, that eternity has this Bride at its very centre. Somehow we need to understand what it means to prepare ourselves as the Bride of Christ, to get ourselves ready. I hope this book will contribute to that process of preparation.

As I begin this book, reflecting on 47 years of passionately, if not perfectly, pursuing a vision for Jesus' church, his Bride, I feel I am trying to do the impossible. I'm trying to do justice to something that is so wonderful, so glorious, so incredible, so indescribable, so diverse, so complex, so multifaceted, so amazing, that it required the death of God's son to bring it into existence. And in fact it has taken 2000 years of twists and turns, ups and downs, and times of great darkness along

---

[1] Rev 19:7 NASB
[2] Rev 21:2 NASB

with times of unbelievable revelation and breakthrough, to get even a glimpse of what this Bride could be like.

A bit of historical context. We planted Frontline Church in Liverpool in 1991. The call to commitment, the willingness to give, serve and sacrifice, and the building of 'community with a cause' all seemed relatively straightforward. It was common for members to volunteer in several ministries as well as be present most Sundays. It was normal for sacrifices to be made to achieve worthy goals. At one point we had 30–40 volunteers visiting 2000 kids in their homes and, of them, 1000 each week being bussed in or walking in to a variety of weekly clubs. People would be out till the early hours serving the homeless with food and drinks. People thought nothing of it.

Our current context.
The incendiary rise of individualism, entitlement and consumerism, and the rapid and radical changes in our society away from its Christian heritage and foundations have left us scratching our heads in a very different landscape. The growth of the Internet, the power of social media, the rise of the thought police[3], and the questioning of all authority has left the church wondering where to go next.

The impact of radical individualism, entitlement, and the subsequent consumerism has in my opinion led to a number of responses from church leaders.

---

[3] In George Orwell's book 1984 the superstate Oceana maintains control over its citizens by monitoring not only what they do, but also what they say, and even think. Hence they are referred to as Thinkpol or the thought police. There are parallels with today's state legislated prohibitions on saying or even thinking certain things that don't adhere to the politically correct liberal elite agenda and dogmas.

One response has been for leaders to bury their heads in the sand and keep doing what they have always done, hoping that things will somehow return to a 'better day'. This response is destined to lead only to extinction.

The second response has been to seek to make the church more attractive to individualistic consumers, with more comfortable buildings, better children's work, lively and loud praise and worship, hipster pastors in skinny jeans sipping on their macchiatos, while preaching their feel-good messages.

Please forgive the slight cynicism. Don't get me wrong, I'm all for church being attractive. Who wants to be part of an unattractive church? But where that has morphed into an appeal to those individualistic consumers, we are on a slippery slope. The moment that another church starts up that does it better, loyalty goes out the window.

A third response, which may or may not include the big gathered expressions of church, will look to reach an unreached, unchurched generation, appealing not to their individualistic consumerism but to their God-given desire for authenticity, belonging in community, and discovery of meaning and purpose. It is this third way that has been my quest for the last 47 years, since the age of 19. It was 1973 when I discovered the joy of mission, the connectedness of community, and the power of discipleship. This started on a summer mission spent with YWAM[4], and was strengthened by joining one of the early house churches in Bristol in the following months.

---

[4] Youth With A Mission.

This third response is the starting point, I believe, for the quest to find and become the church that Jesus died for and is coming back for. The magnificent Bride of Christ.

However what I hear and see when I look around is another story. I feel disappointed and frustrated when I hear comments that echo the consumerist attitude. Comments like:

"I didn't like the worship this morning, I much prefer Andy as a worship leader."

"I'm not sure I want to stay in this church, do you know they have asked me to go on the children's rota twice this month!"

"I don't think I'm going to go to tonight's prayer meeting, I've had a busy day and want to watch another episode of Stranger Things on Netflix."

"I don't like the fact that my church teaches on tithing, I want to decide if I'm going to give or not, and where to."

"Don't ask me to go to a home group, just going on a Sunday once or twice a month is enough."

"I need to do what is right for me."

You get the idea.

Then when I see Christians just cruising from one church to another I feel sad. Sometimes there are good reasons for moving church, but often there is simply an offence that has not been dealt with. We don't do that with our natural family, so why do we feel we have the right to pick and choose our spiritual family. If God has clearly joined us to one local expression of church, there has to be a pretty compelling reason, like abuse, heresy, or moral failure on the part of leaders to move on.

What I have noticed is that when someone has made the move once, it becomes so much easier to do it again. It deepens the individualistic consumer attitude that says 'I have a right to choose a church that is convenient or comfortable for me.' Eventually they become a spiritual gypsy, always on the move, ever more critical, less content, and less likely to have the joy of making any kind of spiritual contribution. It's very sad.

An alternative strap line for this book was 'Bride....why I still love the church....an antidote to today's dismissive, dishonouring and destructive view of church.'

You see Christ and the church are one. You can't love one without the other.

You can't say you love Jesus the Bridegroom, but have no time for the church, his Bride. It's a contradiction in terms.

In trying to explain the relationship between Christ and the church the Apostle Paul uses the metaphor of a bride and bridegroom.

As the Scriptures say, "A man leaves his father and mother and is joined to his wife, and the two are united into one." This is a great mystery, but it is an illustration of the way Christ and the church are one.[5]

So, against this backdrop I find myself compelled to try and articulate something of an apologetic for the glorious church, the beautiful Bride that I think Jesus has in mind when he said '…I will build my church, and the gates of Hades will not overpower it.'[6]

My hope and prayer is that you will be encouraged, uplifted, and perhaps a little challenged to be part of this church, to play your unique part with others in community for the long

---

[5] Eph 5:31-32 NLT
[6] Matt 16:18 NASB

haul. I pray that it will help to grow in you a clear and compelling vision that helps you to keep going when you experience the inevitable setbacks. The church is made up of broken people, so let's not expect everything in church to be perfect. That is reserved for heaven!

As always, I find it essential to combine vision with action, inspiration with perspiration, 'why to' with 'how to'. So as well as lots of practical content, I also want to invite you to consider two or three questions at the end of each chapter, either for personal reflection, or group discussion.

So the book can be used as a discussion starter for leadership teams who are looking for more, or for small groups that are trying to figure out how they can be a more rich and dynamic expression of church.

Konrad Adenauer, a former West German Chancellor said 'We all live under the same sky, but we don't all have the same horizon.' May your horizon be expanded in the reading of this book.

The Journey

As I have studied church history over many years, I have found not a random series of stops and starts, or chaotic initiatives, but a story of God at work, continually preparing a Bride for his Son, the Bridegroom.

Let me pick up the story in the book of Acts.

The Apostle Peter, with John, has just healed the man at Gate Beautiful. He preaches a sermon to the gathered crowds and says,

Therefore repent and return, so that your sins may be wiped away, in order that times of refreshing may come from the presence of the Lord; and that He may send Jesus, the Christ appointed for you, whom heaven must receive until the period of restoration of all things about which God spoke by the mouth of His holy prophets from ancient time.[7]

I believe that this period of restoration is the time we are now living in. It is this present age, which as theologian George Eldon Ladd says, overlaps with the age to come.[8] The kingdom is breaking in, as God's people 'seek first the kingdom' and pray daily 'your kingdom come'.

This period of restoration is the time we are now living in.

Let me try rewriting that passage in Amplified style (my wording):

Therefore repent, change your mind and orientation, and return to the Lord with all your heart, so that your sins may be wiped away, giving you clear access to the Father and an open heaven for his blessing;
....in order that times, (Greek– Kairoses[9]*), opportunities, those moments of the kingdom breaking in that lead to specific seasons of refreshing, may come from the presence of the Lord and His Spirit;*
....and that He may send Jesus, the Christ, the anointed one, appointed for you, His precious child, whom heaven must receive, following His ascension, until the period of time,

---

[7] Acts 3:19-21 NASB

[8] George Eldon Ladd, A Theology of the New Testament, James Clarke and Co Ltd

[9] The Greek word for time here is *Kairos*. It is a breaking-in moment of time, a specific opportunity for the kingdom to be experienced. Mark 1:15 speaks about this.

(Greek– Chronos[10]), the gradual restoration of all things which will be finally and fully revealed in heaven, about which God spoke by the mouth of His holy prophets from ancient time, since the beginning of the world.[11]

We can confidently say that this period of restoration is not just the final moment of revelation of the coming kingdom, but the ongoing breaking in of God's kingdom in the here and now.

What's my point? It's this, that since the death and resurrection of Christ, and the birth of the church on the day of Pentecost, we have been living in this period of restoration of all things. We see the lifestyle and impact of a devoted, dynamic, dazzling early church that maintained its vigour and purity for the first 300 years. After that followed 1000 years of decline, depravity and deception. There is a reason we call it 'the Dark Ages'.

This darkness was punctuated by the light of a number of radical breakaway movements. The light of Christ in the church was kept alive by small bands of believers who refused to bow to the weight and authority of a corrupt and compromised institutional church. These prophetic communities were often ostracised and persecuted, frequently living in extended family groups outside the mainstream, but they were also outward focused, being salt and light in the world, against the backdrop of a spiritually impotent church. They were the hope of a church still to come.

---

[10] The Greek word for time or period here is *Chronos*. It refers to the passing of time, a period of time, rather than a moment in time.

[11] Acts 3:19-21 Nic's wording

Then came the pre-reformation movements like the followers of Peter Waldo in Lyons in the 1100s, John Wycliffe in Oxford in the 1300s, Czech followers of Jan Huss in the 1400s, leading eventually to the main protestant reformation of Luther, Zwingli and Calvin across Europe in the 1500s.

This breaking away from the many unscrupulous practices and false beliefs of the Roman Catholic Church was, at that time, understandably a great threat to the establishment. The Protestant movement confronted the corrupt practice of priests selling indulgences (permits given by priests for payment that supposedly reduced the time spent in purgatory after death); they promoted faith not works as the basis for salvation; and they defined scripture not the Pope as the final authority in matters of faith and praxis. These were all key points of distinction.

But this was just the start of the 'period of restoration of all things'. The Anabaptists, starting with Zwingli, believed in and practised believer's baptism (as opposed to infant baptism). In the 1700's The Moravians in Herrnhut in Germany saw a restoration of Holy Spirit

The Moravians in Herrnhut in Germany saw a restoration of Holy Spirit renewal, global missions, and continuous prayer.

renewal, global missions, and continuous prayer. John Wesley and the Methodist revival in the UK built on this in the same century, seeing a restoration of discipleship practices, church planting, and social care of local communities, for example, in education, medical care and in supporting the abolition of slavery.

In the 1800s the Salvation Army, growing out of Methodism, started to build a whole movement based on God's kingdom people living as soldiers of Christ, preaching the gospel, starting new mission bases, caring for the poorest and most broken in society, the homeless and hungry, and addressing the deeper injustices in society such as factory reform and helping create employment.

Other pioneer groups emerged working with children and in other areas of social justice. These included the City Mission movement, the Shaftesbury Society, Barnardo's and Muller's orphanages. This spilled over into the 1900s.

Then in God's timetable for the restoration of all things, a Holy Spirit explosion took place in Azusa Street in Los Angeles in the USA, and rapidly spread around the globe. Based on an expectation of the experience of the baptism of the Holy Spirit, the Assemblies of God, Foursquare and Elim among many other Pentecostal denominations began to emerge. All of these were accompanied by a new manifestation of the gifts of the Spirit, healings and miracles.

In the second half of the 1900s, the Pentecostal movement began to infuse mainstream denominations, with many embracing charismatic experiences. This also paved the way for the house church movement. House churches were often started when their founders experienced the baptism of the Holy Spirit, speaking in tongues and the other spiritual gifts.

Where established churches resisted this move, many were forced to move out and start new churches. These often began in homes, and hence the house church movement of the 1960s and 70s. Through these, there was a renewed emphasis on every member ministry (as there had been through the Brethren movement in the early 1900s). Home-based groups of believers shared life together and built community at a local level. Fresh creativity in music led to new styles of praise and worship.

In the 1980s John Wimber with his West Coast USA laid-back style, and his attractiveness to Anglican and other mainstream denominations in the UK, brought respectability to healing ministry and spiritual gifts. What had been a small minority of renewed Anglicans within the Fountain Trust under the direction of Michael Harper in the 1960s started to become mainstream, especially with the ever-increasing influence of Holy Trinity Brompton Church in London.

Many of the new practices, which developed within what was essentially a breakaway house church movement, eventually became normal in most denominations; the house church movement morphed into the new church movement as the 1900s came to a close.

As you can see there has been an amazing period of restoration of all things.

Globally, the 2000s have seen the emergence of the missional movement, disciple-making movements and rapidly multiplying church-planting movements, the latter especially in Asia and the global south. The worldwide church has never been more exciting or growing faster.

Unfortunately this has not yet permeated into the western church to any great extent. Signs of hope are there. There are green shoots emerging, but this is not a time to rest on our laurels. We need to push harder and faster into Jesus' vision for his church. We must not accept the few examples of growing churches as an indication that we are doing well.

In the UK, as in the US, church attendance statistics show an overall decline[12], which will eventually mean the closure of many churches. There are pockets of growth, especially in

---

[12] 'Most key measures of attendance in the Church of England fell by between 10% and 20% from 2008 to 2018'. Taken from Church of England research and statistics. Statistics for Mission 2018.
https://www.churchofengland.org/sites/default/files/2019-10/2018StatisticsForMission_0.pdf

the black and Asian churches, and in some of the newer expressions of church. And we've yet to fully discover the overall impact of Covid-19 and lockdown on church growth, both the positive and the negative.[13]

Hundreds if not thousands more churches will close in the next 20 years. Will we wake up to the challenge of church in the 21st century, or will we just hold on stubbornly to our ticket to heaven, while the vast majority of the population is alienated from church and unaware of the good news of Jesus and his kingdom?

The Structure

As we explore what this church, that Jesus died for and is coming back for, looks like, the word BRIDE will shape our thinking. We will dig into different aspects of the Bride, the greatest love of the Bridegroom. Each chapter will address the questions below, in both personal and corporate dimensions. The questions following each section of each chapter will help focus our reflections, stir us to action and compile responses to shape our best contribution to his church in the future.

This is the outline of the next 5 sections:

B: Burning with desire – how can we grow in our love for Jesus, so that it is the motivation for everything else we do, avoiding the traps of pressure to perform, legalism and dutiful obligation?

---

[13] See Covid-19 addendum

R: Radical community – how are we meant to live differently from the culture around us? What does Jesus' community look like? How do we break down our conformity to our culture?

I: Invincible army – how does being an army shape how we think of ourselves and act together? What are some keys to the successful enforcement of our victory in Christ?

D: Disciple-making disciples – how does this priority infiltrate and affect everything we do? How do we step towards authentic disciple-making movements?

E: End-times perspective – what are our expectations of Christ's kingdom before he returns, and how does the return of Christ keep us going and inform our purpose and priorities in this life?

Questions:

- What issues might tempt you to be a bit cynical about church?

- Do you notice your own responses or attitudes being about personal preferences? If so, which particular aspects of church draw out the consumer in you?

- To what extent have you seen yourself as part of a global historic movement of restoration that is moving towards a conclusion at Christ's return?

- Do you enjoy challenge and change, or do you prefer the safety and security of what is known?

Part 1 – Burning With Desire

The Bride is made up of individual followers, lovers of Jesus. The Apostle Peter asks this question in the light of the return of Christ the Bridegroom.

…what sort of people ought you to be in holy conduct and godliness, looking for and hastening the coming of the day of God…[1]

'What sort of people ought we to be?' Well, we need to be many things, but first of all we need to be a people who are 'burning with desire'. Everything starts here. Without a heart motivation of love everything is reduced to duty and obligation.

Without a heart motivation of love everything is reduced to duty and obligation.

In the Apostle John's Revelation of the end times, culminating with the return of the Bridegroom for his Bride[2], Jesus has some harsh words to say to the seven churches in Asia Minor (modern day western Turkey).[3] Out of those seven churches, five were falling short of Jesus' expectation. Sardis had a name for being alive but was dead[4], Laodicea was described as being lukewarm, worthy only of being spat

---

[1] 2 Pet 3:11-12 NASB
[2] Rev 22:16-20
[3] Rev 2 & 3
[4] Rev 3:1

out or vomited up[5], and Ephesus, the jewel in the crown of the early church's apostolic centres, was told that they had left their first love and were in danger of having their lampstand removed (snuffed out).[6]

This issue of first love is so important. We can't move forward till we have addressed the issue of lack of zeal (burning desire) in the church. Ephesus was called to repent and return to doing those things it did at first.[7] They were called back to the passion and purity of the earliest expressions of the church.[8] This is one of the reasons we keep coming back to the early church's pattern and lifestyle in considering how we become 'the church that Jesus died for and is coming back for', the glorious Bride!

---

[5] Rev 3:16
[6] Rev 2:4
[7] Rev 2:5
[8] Acts 2:42-47, Acts 19:1-20

Chapter 1

Falling in love

How do we grow our love for Jesus so that it is the motivation for everything else?

Most brides want to be in love with their beloved bridegroom, and they want their bridegroom to be in love with them too. To love and be loved is at the heart of the human longing.

I wonder if some of us feel that this marriage is more like an arranged marriage than one based on mutual love. I once had a dream after watching a particular episode of the TV series Poldark. In the dream I found myself trapped in an arranged, loveless marriage (as one of the characters was in that particular episode). It was not a dream but a nightmare! I know of several arranged Asian marriages that are brilliant, but this one in the dream definitely wasn't.

We don't have much trouble believing in theory that Jesus our bridegroom loves us; but do we really know it by experience, rather than just through good theology? What we do know is that he demonstrates his love for us supremely by dying on the cross for us.

But God showed his great love for us by sending Christ to die for us while we were still sinners.[1]

---

[1] Rom 5:8 NLT

Luke reports this heart cry of Jesus in the Garden of Gethsemane as he faced the prospect of death:

"Father, if you are willing, please take this cup of suffering away from me. Yet I want your will to be done, not mine."[2]

Everything within Jesus wanted to find another way to obey the Father, but Jesus' willingness to go to the cross, against his natural inclination, is astounding. He desperately wanted to avoid the cross, yet for your sake and mine, he went through the physical agony of crucifixion and the spiritual agony of separation from his Father. It is astounding, not only that he would die for good people, but that he would also die for the rapist, the paedophile, the bigot, the racist, the thief, the swindler and the most hate-filled murderer. That kind of love is pretty hard to get our heads round.

Most of us who have children feel extremely protective of them, we could even imagine sacrificing our lives for them under certain circumstances. That's because we see them as our dearly loved precious children, made in our image and so a part of us. God also sees all of us as his children. He feels the same about each one of us. We may not all have acknowledged him as our father, and so appropriated our adoption as daughters and sons yet, but that doesn't change how he sees us. Remarkable!

For some reason Jesus seems to find us irresistible, even at our worst.

I sometimes say that 'it's hard to resist someone who finds you irresistible'. For some reason Jesus seems to find us irresistible, even at our worst.

---

[2] Lk 22:42 NLT

Why is it so important to know 'by experience' that we are loved by him? The Apostle John says;

We love Him, because He first loved us.[3]

It's because his love for us is the source of all love, both for him, and for others. We cannot truly know love for others, or sustain love for him without first knowing by experience how much he loves us. Our reflex response to this love is the motivation for all we do.

The alternatives are doing things because of duty, fear, guilt or the need to please people or gain their approval. These are all bad reasons for doing anything. God's kingdom is a kingdom based on love, because he is love. He is Jehovah Nissi, 'The Lord is my Banner'[4], our victory banner, and that banner over us is love.[5] We are made in his image and therefore designed supremely to run on love. His love is our fuel cell, and there is an unlimited supply.

Imagine an electric car that is designed to run on clean, renewable energy, a car that has solar panels built in, that constantly recharge its batteries. It never runs out of energy, never pollutes the atmosphere and never depletes our planet of its natural resources. It is powered by the sun, an inexhaustible supply of energy. Well, we are designed to be powered by the Son, an inexhaustible supply of love. All other motivations deplete us or damage those around us

When Jesus saw the crowds of lost people he was moved with compassion.[6] We need to be connected with the love of God if we are going to share in his compassion for people

---

[3] 1 Jn 4:19 AMPC
[4] Ex 17:15
[5] Song of Songs 2:4
[6] Matt 9:36

and situations. I remember when I was visited in my office by a Congolese man called Illilo. He had come to the UK looking for his wife from whom he had been separated in the conflicts that have devastated the Democratic Republic of Congo (DRC). On his way he had gone searching for her in the displacement camps in Kenya; and then, via one of the aid agencies, had been directed to the UK. Eventually he found Nafisa in Liverpool and the two of them had started to worship with us at Frontline Church.

On his way through Kenya he had come across some projects working with orphans, and he came to my office to see if we as a church would be interested in working with orphans in Africa. Up till this point the conversation had been quite normal, pleasant and informative. Then suddenly I felt this overwhelming sense of pity and compassion for the orphans in Africa. I burst into tears. I don't think he was expecting that, and I certainly wasn't.

This began a long journey of working with Illilo and then connecting with various leaders first in Uganda, and then in the DRC. I visited this amazingly beautiful and yet ravaged nation seven or eight times before handing the project on to other leaders in Frontline.

Our trips led to the development of many compassion-based projects in the eastern part of the DRC, in the war-torn province of North Kivu. These included helping a school to be rebuilt and underwriting some of the school fees through child sponsorship, supporting a nursery and families looking after orphans, training counsellors of rape victims (rape was a regular weapon of war by the militias), fundraising for a microfinance organisation helping new business projects get started, support and training for church leaders, evangelism training, and health initiatives, all in the city of Butembo; and eventually the funding and building of a medical and midwifery clinic in Kasindi, along with work in that town with internally displaced people.

15 years on the mayor of Kinshasa, the capital, having heard of our work, is pursuing a formal link with the City of Liverpool's Mayor, and at the time of writing is working towards a delegation coming to visit the Mayor and his staff in our city to build stronger links.

All this began because of one deeply felt, unexpected moment of compassion for the needs of African children. Who knows where love will lead?

Imagine a church of women and men who have truly connected with the love of God, who are fuelled by that love, and willing to pay whatever it takes to be pleasing to 'him who loved us and gave his life for us'.[7] These are lives lived from constant gratitude. They are lives marked by the love that he demonstrated at the cross. Following Jesus involves both commitment and cost and we will only sustain these when we are both love motivated and love powered. This is his plan.

That's why we need to know the love of God, the grace of the Lord Jesus Christ, and the fellowship of the Holy Spirit.[8] It's our rocket fuel.

Are we talking about emotions here? Sadly so many of us are hostage to our emotions. Emotions are not bad, but they are not good barometers of truth, guides for decision-making, or motivation for action. They come and go. They simply reflect how we are feeling, nothing more and nothing less. But I believe that our emotions are responsive to our beliefs, words (confessions) and actions. They will eventually come into line with our confessed beliefs and aligned actions. So it is possible to live in a way that restores emotional depletion,

---

[7] Gal 2:20, Eph 5:2
[8] 2 Cor 13:14

corrects emotional depression, and imparts emotional satisfaction and joy.

So it is possible to live in a way that restores emotional depletion, corrects emotional depression, and imparts emotional satisfaction and joy.

Don't imagine that I believe all emotional problems have a purely spiritual answer! I have no problem with the use of antidepressants. In my days as a GP I prescribed them regularly and know they are very helpful in the right circumstances. I have personally benefited from counselling and have often been heard to say 'everyone needs counselling!' But in today's 'therapy culture', medication and counselling are often the first, and possibly only port of call, rather than first turning to be loved by God and restored by that love.

So knowing how important receiving and responding to his love is, how do we position ourselves for that love, how do we align ourselves with his love? How does Jesus become our passion, our desire, our priority and our delight?
The following chapters will outline a few different ways we can do that.

Questions:

- Are we more motivated in serving God through duty or delight, guilt or gratitude, fear or in response to his favour?
- What do we do when our emotions are telling us to give up, to withdraw, to let our anger loose, or to indulge ourselves?

Chapter 2

Creating Visceral Connections

Some years ago God got my attention when he pointed out that whenever I was praying I was more interested in transaction than connection. In other words I was hoping that if I did or said the right things in prayer that God would give me what I asked for. It was transactional, not primarily relational. I needed to relearn how to re-connect with him at a visceral (gut) level.

Thus began a quest to rediscover God's presence, love and leading in prayer. The journey involved a lot of praise and worship, a lot of confessing my sins and declaring truths about God, a lot of gratitude prayers, and a lot of praying and singing in tongues. Gradually, over a 6-month period, I discovered a new sense of his presence, his delight and his love as I spent time set aside with him. Out of this came a new desire for time in his presence, a new clarity in my praying, a new energising of those prayers and a new authority in standing against the schemes of the enemy in prayer.

Desire and delight became the hallmarks of my time with God. No more duty or worse still drudgery! I looked forward to spending time with him, in his word, in worship, in listening and in prayer. I still do. Learning to make the visceral connection was key.

Desire and delight became the hallmarks of my time with God.

I deliberately use the word visceral to describe something that is more than intellectual, and more than emotional. It is a kind of 'deep calling to deep' that the psalmist spoke of.[1] In the medical world the viscera are our internal organs. The King James Version of the Bible often uses the word 'bowels' to describe our innermost being, our heart, our inner (wo)man, or spirit. So a visceral connection makes sense from a biblical point of view as well.

Jesus was frequently described as being 'moved with compassion'. The word for this is usually the Greek word 'splagchnizomai' which literally means 'to have the bowels yearn'. In the culture of Jesus' day, the bowels were thought to be the seat of love and pity. That Greek word is also where we get the medical word splanchnic from, describing anything relating to the internal organs. So much medical and Greek information!

So when I say 'making a visceral connection', I hope you have a bit more of a sense of what I'm talking about. Literally it is a 'gut-level' connection. It has elements of intuition, conviction, emotion, affection and passion, as well as connection to his presence.

These kind of connections are vital to a healthy, glowing Bride that is fuelled by love, a body that can keep giving out without giving up[2], a temple that is constantly filled with his presence[3], an army that can withstand all the attacks of the enemy[4], and a family that is held together by cords of love.[5] These are the five primary images for the church in the book of Ephesians – the household or temple in chapter 2, a family

---

[1] Ps 42:7
[2] Eph 4:11-16
[3] Eph 2:19-22
[4] Eph 6:10-13
[5] Eph 3:14-19

in chapter 3, a body in chapter 4, a bride in chapter 5, and an army in chapter 6.

When it comes to building a love foundation and motivation for the Bride to live and work together as one, then those 'times of refreshing from the presence of the Lord'[6] that we spoke about earlier are vital. Although I love to spend time on my own worshipping God, I really appreciate the opportunities to come together in homes and in our bigger gatherings to worship God, all of these so much missed at the time of writing, due to lockdown restrictions.

There is something very unifying, to all be focussed on the one we love at the same time, raising our voices, and directing our hearts to the king of love, allowing the beauty of his presence to melt our cold hearts and heal our wounded souls. It is often the moment when I find tears of gratitude and love welling up. And for someone who doesn't tend to display emotion much, that is quite significant.

It's all too easy to do lip service to our sung worship, and just go through the motions till we get to the meat of the word in the preach, or for some of us it's the coffee afterwards! If we are having trouble connecting with the Lord in sung worship, then as well as using our minds to understand the words that are being sung, let me encourage you to try using your imaginations to connect with ideas, images and situations that the words we are singing bring to mind. I guarantee it will enrich your experience and help orcate that visceral connecllon.

Visceral connections are also strengthened by the 'fellowship of the Holy Spirit'.[7] This fellowship is the Greek word 'koinonia', which unpacked means our constant friendship

---

[6] Acts 3:19 NASB
[7] 2 Cor 13:14

and partnership with him. It's being in contact throughout our day, through simply being mindful that he is with us always.[8] It's quietly speaking in tongues when that's possible. It is sending up short arrow prayers. It's singing love songs to him while doing more menial tasks. It's asking him to be present with us, to give us help in particular situations. It's responding to the nudges of his leading.[9] And it's developed in many other ways.

Take delight in the Lord, and he will give you your heart's desires.[10]

Questions:

- How often do you spend dedicated time with God, where you can focus exclusively on him and his love for you? Is this satisfying for you?
- Do your prayer times create visceral connections with God, or are they more transactional, if so what might you do to change that?
- How, when and where do you experience the fellowship of the Holy Spirit?

———————————————————

[8] Matt 28:20
[9] Rom 8:14
[10] Ps 37:4 NLT

Chapter 3

Repentance, the joy-filled life

This was the title of a small book by Basilea Schlink1 that I read in my 20s. It intrigued me that something that seemed so negative – repentance, could lead to something so positive – joy.

Over the decades since, it has proved to be true time and time again. In fact I've sometimes toyed with the idea that it's almost worth sinning just to experience the joy of repentance (not really!).

It's almost worth sinning just to experience the joy of repentance (not really!).

Repentance and receiving forgiveness are keys to growing in desire for God. They cleanse our souls from the detritus of bad decisions and of compromised relationships. Of unkind words spoken in haste and of pleasures sought outside of the will of God. Of the failure to seek first the kingdom, and much more.

It's more than just keeping short accounts with God over sins of commission or omission; it's a way of life. Living in repentance and forgiveness is the antidote to self-righteousness, guilt and shame. Living in forgiveness is a key to burning with desire for the Lord. It produces a profound

[1] Basilea Schlink, Repentance the Joy-filled Life, Kanaan Publications.

gratitude and humility, both of which are essential ingredients to the recipe for living in love.

Imagine the scene, Jesus is having a meal with a religious and probably somewhat self-righteous leader called Simon.[2] He has other special guests who are also keen to meet this Jesus. Simon is probably quite proud of the fact that Jesus, the renowned teacher-healer-prophet, has chosen to eat with him.

Enter a local woman of dubious reputation (probably a prostitute) from the town. She slips in behind the honoured guests who are reclining at table and she starts to do something no one else but Jesus would have tolerated. She lets her tears wash Jesus' feet. There are murmurs around the room, quiet nudges, 'Do you see what she is doing?' Not only is she wetting his feet with her tears, but she is wiping them dry with her hair. Her hair, which should have been covered in polite society, is hanging loose, and would have been seen by the guests as a sign of her promiscuity. Having dried his feet with her hair, she then anoints them with precious and expensive oil from her alabaster jar, moisturising the dry skin from a day's walking in dusty territory.

You could cut the atmosphere in the room with a knife. All eyes are on Simon the host, to see what he will do or say. In the end only his words to himself are recorded for us. He cannot believe that Jesus could really be a prophet if he was allowing this woman to do this highly inappropriate, scandalous thing. Jesus, knowing Simon's musing and mutterings, confronts him in his critical thoughts by telling them all a story about two debtors, one with a huge unpayable debt (equivalent to two years' wages), the other with a much smaller one. Both debtors have their debts

---

[2] Luke 7:36-50

cancelled. Which of them, Jesus asks, would be the most grateful, which would love their benefactor more? Clearly it's the one with the greater debt. Jesus goes on to make the point...

"Therefore, I tell you, her many sins have been forgiven—as her great love has shown. But whoever has been forgiven little loves little."[3]

The point is clear, we love in proportion to the knowledge and experience of our forgiveness. If the Bride is going to be burning with desire, she needs to fall in love with her Bridegroom all over again through the regular experience of his forgiveness in response to her repentance.

> *We love in proportion to the knowledge and experience of our forgiveness.*

While I don't encourage digging for dirt in accounting for sin in our relationship with God, I do encourage moments of reflection and listening to the small, loving, convicting voice of the Holy Spirit when we spend time with God. Is there anything I need to repent of and ask forgiveness for? If so, don't hide from the Lord in shame, like Adam and Eve in the Garden of Eden, [4] but run into his arms, ask for his forgiveness and wallow in his love!

Questions:

- Does shame about your thoughts, words or deeds drive you to run towards God's loving forgiveness or away from it?

---

[3] Luke 7:47
[4] Gen 3:8

- When was the last time you experienced the joy of repentance?

Chapter 4

Making Good Investments

Jesus said,

"Do not store up for yourselves treasures on earth, where moths and vermin destroy, and where thieves break in and steal. But store up for yourselves treasures in heaven, where moths and vermin do not destroy, and where thieves do not break in and steal. For where your treasure is, there your heart will be also."[1]

'Where your treasure is, that's where your heart will be.' This issue of what motivates us is so important. If we are to be the Bride of Christ, burning with desire for our Bridegroom, then we have to attend to our hearts, the seat of desire and motivation.

When I was younger and we used to visit my wife, Jenny's mum and dad, her dad had two particular areas of interest that meant very little to me. They were the stock market and horse racing! It made conversation and building our relationship hard work. Why was he so passionate about those two interests? Because that's where he made his investments. That's where his treasure was, and that's where his heart was. First thing in the morning he would check the papers to see what the stock market was doing. He would read all the financial reports of the companies he had

---

[1] Matt 6:19-21

invested in. He researched potential future investments. It was his passion. He was deeply invested in it, not just financially, but also emotionally, and with his time and energy. It was what he wanted to talk about.

> *Where are we putting our treasure, what are we investing in?*

Jesus is clear, wherever we invest our treasure – that's where our heart will be. Where are we putting our treasure, what are we investing in?

Later in the same chapter Jesus said we were to seek first the Kingdom of God.[2] What does that mean? Does it mean we become 'so heavenly minded that we are no earthly use?' I don't think so. Jesus is looking for people who not only have their head in the clouds, seeking those things that are above,[3] but also have their feet firmly on the ground. Those who understand how the world works, and who are deeply invested in their family, community, school, workplace, and town or city.

It's not an easy balance to get right. Most of us have met overly spiritual people who sometimes make bad decisions for a lack of good old-fashioned common sense. It's true that that common sense is actually remarkably uncommon.

We also know that there are those who are so 'grounded' that the thought of praying about something they are dealing with rarely occurs to them. They can easily resort to depending on their own resources, gifts and experience. They don't tend to go to God unless all natural resources have failed them. God has become the option of last resort. I wonder how God feels about that.

---

[2] Matt 6:33
[3] Col 3:1

So if investments are key, what do we invest in? Jesus makes it pretty simple when he tells us to seek his kingdom first. But what does that actually mean?

The kingdom is mentioned 126 times in the gospels and 34 times in the rest of the New Testament. So it has to be pretty important. Jesus actually taught his disciples to pray 'your kingdom come, your will be done on earth as it is in heaven'.

John Piper defines the kingdom of God (and of heaven) as God's kingly rule — his reign, his action, his lordship, his sovereign governance.[4]

If the kingdom is the rule of God, then we are invited in the Lord's Prayer to join with every other believer in praying for that rule to be extended on earth, as it is perfectly expressed in heaven. So seeking first the kingdom is to seek to bring his rule into every area of life. First and foremost into our own lives as we live lives of surrender to his kingship; and then the lives of others who don't yet know his saving, healing, restoring, rescuing power. This happens when those who don't know him turn from the domain of darkness to the kingdom of light.[5] But it's also bringing his rule into my family, my community, my school, my workplace, and the culture of my town or city.

We do this by being good news people wherever we go. We bring the good news of God's kingdom in our words, our actions, through our prayers, and our godly influence wherever God places us.

---

[4] From John Piper's website 'Desiring God' https://www.desiringgod.org/interviews/what-is-the-kingdom-of-god
[5] I Peter 2:9

In each situation ask him 'how can I bring your kingdom here?'

So seeking first the kingdom means a myriad of different things in our different contexts. It may help us to consider a simple question to help us figure out what seeking and bringing the kingdom in any particular place might look like. We can ask God to use us each day to be kingdom ambassadors, and then in each situation ask him 'how can I bring your kingdom here?' It's not rocket science, is it?

It may be:
- by serving well
- by a word of encouragement
- through a shared testimony
- by an act of kindness
- by giving a gift
- through an intercessory prayer
- by bringing peace to a tense workplace environment
- by reconciling two people who are out of sorts with each other
- by standing up for someone being bullied, or in a situation where there is obvious injustice
- by directly talking about Jesus
- by offering to pray with someone who has needs that Jesus can meet.

As you can see, it could be in so many different ways. We just need to ask the question and expect God to show us what to do.

All of these kinds of actions will be an investment in the kingdom. As you make these kinds of investments you will find your heart warmed towards God and you will grow in affection for him. You will find loving him easier and easier. You will grow in the knowledge of his love for you as you feel his pleasure.

The Apostle Paul said that he made it his ambition to be pleasing to God.[6] As we invest in his kingdom, we will be pleasing to him, and will enjoy that sense of his pleasure over us. As we invest in those things he has called us to do, we will enjoy his delight. Eric Liddell, the central character in the film 'Chariots of Fire' competed in the 1924 Olympics before going on to be a missionary. In his early athletics days he famously said "I believe God made me for a purpose, but he also made me fast! And when I run I feel his pleasure."

These kingdom investments may be big or small, but all are of value. All warm our heart. Over the years Jenny and I have had the joy of making some quite significant investments.

The year was 1986 and we had bought a lovely old house in Bristol. I was still a GP (general medical practitioner) and therefore on a good income. I loved the house for its many old features – fireplaces and shutters, and especially for its roof top observatory, an original feature for the person who had commissioned the house's construction in the mid-1800s. The man who was obviously a keen astronomer had built a small flight of stairs from the top landing onto the roof where a small circular room with a dome-shaped rotating roof was located. It had an opening section that would allow a telescope to survey the night skies. Although the dome no longer rotated or opened, it gave brilliant views over the city and provided a great place for prayer.

It was also the largest house we have ever lived in, with eight bedrooms and a self-contained basement flat. At one time there were about 16 of us living there in community. Many happy memories!

But only 18 months after buying it, the Lord asked us to sell it and give half the equity to a Christian school project in our

---

[6] 2 Cor 5:9

city. I still remember the sense of joy, liberation from the power of mammon, and hilarity in giving away what seemed a huge amount of money. It was an investment in the kingdom. It moved my heart more than ever to desire Jesus and his kingdom. It also gave me a real passion for Christian education. Where my investment went, there was my heart also.

The follow-on to that story was that for the next five years we moved into an end-terraced 1960s town house less than half the size, and we were very happy there. This coincided with me giving up full-time medicine, and working fewer and fewer hours in the practice. This was another big kind of investment. After five years of security and success in my own medical practice, I now spent most of my time working in church leadership.

Five years later, the Lord asked us to make another investment, to leave the city of Bristol where we had been living and working for the previous 19 years, and move to the city of Liverpool to plant a new church. The investment in a new city, and in a new church was costly and significant. It involved upheaval for our whole family and the team who came with us, and leaving behind our Bristol vision and the opportunities that we had been cultivating for years. However, once again the investment only made my heart grow more in love with Jesus and his kingdom. And the next couple of decades were full of God's favour and great joy.

The unexpected blessing in it all was that, in moving to Liverpool, we discovered that property prices were half the price of Bristol, and the Lord once again gave us a great house in which we could start the church and build community!

To 'seek first' means to actively pursue, to prioritise, and at times to discipline ourselves for a greater prize than those this world has to offer. As Jesus said, '... what do you benefit if you gain the whole world but lose your own soul?'[7]

To 'seek first' means to actively pursue, to prioritise, and at times to discipline ourselves for a greater prize

To seek first means to ask God for his love, his motivation, his passion and compassion. It means to ask him for his wisdom, his kindness and his courage. It means to ask him each day for opportunities to bring his kingdom to this world, to have the insight to recognise those opportunities, and the boldness to take them when they come.

There are disciplines and habits we can develop to cultivate this as a lifestyle. By my best guess, it takes about six days to build a discipline – in this phase you have to exercise both memory to do it, and the will to do it. It then takes about six weeks to form a habit – where you aren't having to remember as it's now habit, but you still have to exercise choice. After that it's about six months to create a lifestyle – where you neither have to remember or exercise will, it's just what you do! This is the goal!

The Apostle Paul said to Timothy his protégé,

Physical training [bodily discipline in some translations] is good, but training for godliness is much better, promising benefits in this life and in the life to come.[8]

The promise of God is that as we play our part, God will do his in creating desire and love-based motivation for all we do.

---

[7] Mark 8:36 NLT
[8] 1 Tim 4:8 NLT

...Work hard to show the results of your salvation, obeying God with deep reverence and fear. For God is working in you, giving you the desire and the power to do what pleases him.[9]

Or as the Passion Translation puts verse 13,

···God will continually revitalize you, implanting within you the passion to do what pleases him.

Questions:

- When did you last pray about something in the workplace, or about a family or health issue?
- Where are you currently making kingdom investments?
- How is that affecting your heart and motivation?

---

[9] Phil 2:12-13 NLT

Part 2 – Radical Community

Having looked more at individual motivation in Part 1, we will now turn to the first description of the Bride in its corporate expression.

All the believers were one in mind and heart. Selfishness was not a part of their community, for they shared everything they had with one another.[1]

This community is unique, it is counter-cultural, it is the model for a perfect society, neither capitalist nor communist, but kingdom. It is both the highest aspiration for any local church, and the greatest frustration for every local pastor! As I've heard many pastors joke, 'If it wasn't for the people, leading the church would be easy.'

My first experience of what I would later call a missional community was on a houseboat, the Ark, in Amsterdam on a YWAM mission in the summer of 1973. I was there for a month or so between first and second year studies at Medical School.

Each morning we would do our shared jobs. Mine was cleaning the toilets, I seem to remember. On other occasions we painted the outside of the boat together. We then gathered around the scriptures and engaged in growing as disciples, praying for one another and our mission. We shared our food together, and in the afternoon went onto the

---

[1] Acts 4:32 TPT

streets to accost unsuspecting passers-by with a poor explanation of the gospel, often preceded by some truly cringe-worthy street drama! We would invite some back to join us in the evening for coffee where more spiritual conversations would take place, and miraculously some would become followers of Christ. It was all very inspiring, and started to form some of my convictions about the kind of community I believed lay at the heart of Jesus' desire for his church, his Bride.

So what or who are we aspiring to be? What does this radical community look like, and what are the obstacles to seeing its formation?

Chapter 5

A People for God

...you are a chosen people. You are royal priests, a holy nation, God's very own possession. As a result, you can show others the goodness of God, for he called you out of the darkness into his wonderful light.[1]

We will come to the 'showing others the goodness of God' part later. For now, I just want to focus on being God's very own possession, a special, or as the King James translation puts it, a peculiar people (some of us are definitely peculiar). We are first and foremost a radical community set apart for God himself.

For all of eternity, it has been God's desire to have a family. It was in his spiritual DNA if you like, as eternal Father, Son and Holy Spirit. He had no greater desire than to share the perfect

> For all of eternity, it has been God's desire to have a family.

love that they had for each other with us; so that we may not only enjoy that love, but hopefully reciprocate it too. Family is one of the key metaphors for the church in Ephesians.

God is love and is completely self-contained in his love. He needs no one to make him more complete. But the very nature of that love is that it is designed to expand itself and

---

[1] I Pet 2:9 NLT

find more ways to include others. It has unlimited growth potential.

We don't know much about the purpose behind the angelic creation, but it would seem that they had the ability to choose. We know that one third of them rebelled against God and were cast out of heaven.[2] But the creation of mankind was unique. It seems that we had the ability not only to choose, but also to love. What is usually called the great commandment, I think of as God's greatest promise. It was that we would love him with all our heart, mind, and soul[3], the pinnacle of God's creation at the peak of their potential. The God who is love[4], finally finds a fitting family for himself, and a companion Bride for his son, who can love him freely and fully. Wow! No wonder 'the whole creation is on tiptoe to see the wonderful sight of the sons of God coming into their own.'[5]

So we are first and foremost a people for God, for his own possession; a people who he is jealous for. He is jealous in the sense of prizing our exclusive relationship; a relationship uncompromised by the worship of and allegiance to other so-called gods, which are in fact idols.

Our response to this invitation is not one of suspicion, fearing being controlled, but one of delight, that someone so incredible should be so in love with us. Someone who is so powerful wanting to care for, provide for and protect us. Someone so focussed on our well being who is willing to turn every situation, even those where we have messed up, into an opportunity for blessing and prospering us.[6]

---

[2] Ezek 28:13-17, Rev 12:4,9
[3] Matt 22:37
[4] I Jn 4:16
[5] Rom 8:19 J.B.Phillips
[6] Rom 8:28

So we gladly respond to this invitation to be one of his people. We embrace all the challenges and potential for misunderstanding by those around us, even the possibility of persecution by hostile powers that hate our distinctiveness, our moral values and unbending faith. And so in many parts of the world, our sisters and brothers who are part of this 'people for himself' are truly suffering for his name, for their affiliation to his body, his church, in the hope of becoming his Bride. Many have lost, and others continue to lose, their lives rather than deny him or disassociate from his people.

The challenge is to trust in his goodness, his power and his unfailing purpose for our lives. As Job, who had suffered more than most said, 'I know that you can do all things and that no purpose of yours

Learning to trust him is one of our greatest challenges

can be thwarted.'[7]. That lesson in learning to trust him is one of our greatest challenges, and a life-long lesson.

Questions:

- How much do we see our primary identity as 'one of God's people'?
- Consider the story of Daniel's three friends, Shadrach, Meshach and Abednego in Daniel chapter 3. Do we trust God and still identify with him even when it might be expedient to stay silent?

---

[7] Job 42:2 NASB

Chapter 6

A Counter-Cultural Community

This immediately gets to the heart of two big challenges the church faces. The first is our idolatry, our infatuation with the gods of this world, our cultural idols. We've just been seeing that Jesus is jealous for us, to have us for himself, and not to share us with other so-called gods. The second challenge is that our counter-cultural community also takes us full tilt into the extreme discomfort we feel when our distinctive nature is out of kilter with the culture around us.

We are called to be distinctive, and yet we so long to 'fit in' to our workplace, friendship group, gym, club, pub, university or local community. We are not called to fit in, but to stand out like Abraham,

> *We are called to be distinctive, and yet we so long to 'fit in'*

who was described as living in the Promised Land as a stranger, an alien, a foreigner, an immigrant, a temporary resident.[1] The message is clear, we are not meant to see this world as our permanent home, but are to see ourselves as passing through it. Abraham was always looking for something more permanent.

---

[1] Heb 11:9

Abraham was confidently looking forward to a city with eternal foundations, a city designed and built by God.[2]

In the Epistle to Diognetus, the author known only as Mathetes wrote this:[3]

'For the Christians are distinguished from other men neither by country, nor language, nor the customs which they observe. For they neither inhabit cities of their own, nor employ a peculiar form of speech, nor lead a life which is marked out by any singularity. The course of conduct which they follow has not been devised by any speculation or deliberation of inquisitive men; nor do they, like some, proclaim themselves the advocates of any merely human doctrines. But, inhabiting Greek as well as barbarian cities, according as the lot of each of them has determined, and following the customs of the natives in respect to clothing, food, and the rest of their ordinary conduct, they display to us their wonderful and confessedly striking method of life. They dwell in their own countries, but simply as sojourners. As citizens, they share in all things with others, and yet endure all things as if foreigners. Every foreign land is to them as their native country, and every land of their birth as a land of strangers.'

Isn't that a brilliant description of God's pilgrim people, God's radical community, Jesus' Bride?

---

[2] Heb 11:10 NLT

[3] The letter to Diognetes was discovered in a 13thC codex (manuscript book). Many copies were made but the original was then lost in a fire. Nothing is known about Diognetes and it may in fact be a generic name as it simply means God-born. The author known only as Mathetes is probably also a descriptive name as it just means disciple, or student. It is an early example of early church apologetics written in the 2nd or 3rd century.

We are meant to engage with our world, but not to become part of it. Jesus prayed to the Father for us like this:

'I'm not asking you to take them out of the world, but to keep them safe from the evil one. They do not belong to this world any more than I do.'[4]

The evil one, Satan, delights in trapping us in the world's ways, its values, and addiction to its idols. Our idols may not be carved wooden images, but they are every bit as real, and every bit as powerful. They almost certainly represent some of those 'rulers, authorities, cosmic powers over this present darkness, and the spiritual forces of evil in the heavenly places'[5], that the Apostle Paul speaks of when he writes to the church in Ephesus.

The early church was totally counter-cultural. They lived differently. They refused to bow down to Caesar. They didn't adopt the immoral standards of the Greek or Roman culture that surrounded them. Instead they lived

The early church was totally counter-cultural.

as a radical community and extended family. Just read again the description of the early church in Acts 2:

Every believer was faithfully devoted to following the teachings of the apostles. Their hearts were mutually linked to one another, sharing communion and coming together regularly for prayer. A deep sense of holy awe swept over everyone, and the apostles performed many miraculous signs and wonders. All the believers were in fellowship as one body, and they shared with one another whatever they had. Out of generosity they even sold their assets to

---

[4] Jn 17:15-16 NLT
[5] Eph 6:12 ESV

distribute the proceeds to those who were in need among them. Daily they met together in the temple courts and in one another's homes to celebrate communion. They shared meals together with joyful hearts and tender humility. They were continually filled with praises to God, enjoying the favour of all the people. And the Lord kept adding to their number daily those who were coming to life.[6]

I never seem to tire of reading that description. I am bowled over by their commitment to Jesus, raised from the dead; their commitment to each other, sharing all they possessed; and their impact on the world around them.

The Law of First Mention says that whenever something is first mentioned in scripture, there is often a particular significance to that passage. It is usually simple and clear, and contains patterns, blueprints and insights that are vital to future understanding of that topic. This passage is the first description of the church in action, and it is powerful in laying down some of the key principles and practices that we would want to see restored to the church today, if we are to become the Bride of Christ.

You may wonder why they had favour with all the people. Well I can only imagine it was because of the selfless nature of their community and the signs and wonders taking place. It didn't take long however for first the Jews and then the Romans to start persecuting them. Why? Because by their lives they challenged the way of life of those around them.

It's true that our society in the UK loves it when the church runs youth clubs, food banks and street pastors; when they house the homeless, protect the vulnerable, promote fostering and adoption and help those in debt. But society doesn't love our adherence to an exclusive messiah, to

---

[6] Acts 2:42-47 TPT

biblical truth, in fact to any truth that is not willing to bend to the tune of the latest political correctness.

Our power is in our distinctiveness, and in our counter-cultural nature. There are areas where we will stand out as different. Our willingness to forgive rather than hold grudges, and our loving of our enemies. Our refusal to lie even when it is to our own hurt. Our sexual ethics and our commitment to marriage between a man and a woman (which will always get us into trouble). Our view of money and generosity – prioritising loving people and using money, rather than using people and loving money. And in many other ways.

Money of course, in and of itself, is not evil; it is the love of it, the addiction to accumulating it, the using of it purely for ourselves that is the evil part. It was John Wesley who said of money, 'Earn all you can, save all you can, and give all you can.' We cannot all have the resources of a Warren Buffett or Bill Gates to give away, but we can all make sure that the power of mammon (Greek 'mamonas' = riches, worldly wealth)[7] has no hold over us. When was the last time you gave any away, large or small? Generosity is the antidote to the power of mammon.

I still get people look at me as if I am crazy when I pull out a £50 note from my wallet and give it away. I only have it there for that purpose so I'm never tempted to spend it. The joy of giving away, what is in real terms, a relatively small amount of money far outweighs the knowledge that I am £50 poorer as a result! The bank must also wonder who this guy is that keeps coming in asking for £50 notes.

The habit started when Jenny and I got ourselves into a ridiculous amount of debt. We were trying to do God's job for him, by investing in Spanish property to try and create some

---

[7] Matt 6:24

wealth for our pretty pathetic pension fund (an issue for many pastors of my generation). It all went belly-up with the crash in the Spanish property market, and worsened in the next year when the global financial markets had a meltdown. We lost a lot of money. As I reflected on why I had done it (having had clear warning signs from Jenny about doing it), I was forced to admit that there were elements of greed in my motivation, wanting to make a quick buck. There was, as you can imagine, a lot of repenting involved!

As God graciously brought us out of that horrendous situation over the next 10 years, one of the first things he showed me was that I needed to stay free from the fear of lack (one of my Achilles heels), and stay in faith for the finances that he would in time provide. He showed me how to start the £50 note game. And it was, and still does today feel like a game. A game in which I am always the winner! It has largely kept me free from the love of money. It has kept my heart generous. And it helps me to continue to live counter-culturally as part of this radical community, the Bride of Christ.

> *Our use or abuse of money is certainly a good barometer of many other cultural idols.*

They say that a wallet is the nearest thing to a man's heart. Whether that is true or not, our use or abuse of money is certainly a good barometer of many other cultural idols.

Blessing or cursing? Cursing out of frustration or cursing someone who annoys us is pretty ubiquitous. I find it particularly on the road. Maybe it's just my beloved city of Liverpool where people tend to show their feelings and say what they think with little inhibition. This has its up sides and down sides. You always know where you are with people, but there are times when that is a little painful. When I am the cause of someone else's road rage, it is somewhat convicting. I drive with the4points[8] plastered down the side of my car and always feel a little ashamed when my driving gives someone else cause to curse me!

However there are times when I find a similar reaction in myself. Especially when other drivers push in in front of me. Our local High Street is notorious for this particular manoeuvre. So what does counter-cultural look like in this particular instance?

As I asked God about this I felt him encourage me to go in completely the opposite spirit. So my practice for the last few years has been to make it my ambition to deliberately encourage others to pull in in front of me, by leaving space, flashing my lights etc. In my emotional bank account that has now become a win instead of a lose moment. And it is certainly counter-cultural. A small thing in the overall scheme of things, but for me a significant one.

What would it look like for you to be a culture buster in your work place, home life, or social setting?

When all is said and done, we must grow to become committed culture busters if we are to be part of this radical community that is the Bride of Christ. Consider the three big idols of our day, consumerism, individualism and materialism. We need to ask ourselves if we are free from the attraction and addiction to these. We could ask the following questions:

Consumerism – am I more fulfilled by contributing or consuming? Do I expect life to revolve around my convenience and comfort, or around serving others?

---

[8] www.the4points.com

Individualism – Is my family identity more important than my individual pursuit of my rights? Do I make decisions primarily in the light of what is good for me, or what is good for my extended spiritual family?[9]

Materialism – Does giving, rather than getting more stuff give me the joy I seek? Am I protective of my wealth and possessions, wanting to preserve what I have rather than use them to bless others?

These are challenging questions and we tend to be unaware of how our culture's values affect us. It's a bit like the two goldfish swimming in the bowl. One says to the other, 'Wow, the water is cold today isn't it?' The other replies, 'Water, what water?'

When someone from another culture comes into ours, they are much more aware of those things that are contrary to the Bible's teaching and the kingdom's value system. If they come from a developing nation, they can't believe that we put our old people in homes or fail to engage with their wisdom, giving them the respect that is their due. They are shocked that we all live so separately rather than as extended families. They are shocked by our liberal sexual mores and the resultant breakdown of family life.

On the other hand we go to their culture and are shocked by their unwillingness to speak straightforwardly, truthfully and openly about important matters. The result is we are often not sure what they think. We find it hard to do business in such cultures, unsure who we can trust. We are shocked by levels of corruption in government, and the ubiquitous bribery that is a normal part of everyday life.

---

[9] See 'When the Church was a Family' by Joseph H Hellerman, B&H Publishing Group, for more insight into this idea.

It's just the water we swim in.

How much are we conformed to the culture of our world? Where does our thinking need to change? Paul said this to the church in Rome where Greco-Roman culture reigned supreme:

Beloved friends, what should be our proper response to God's marvellous mercies? I encourage you to surrender yourselves to God to be his sacred, living sacrifices. And live in holiness, experiencing all that delights his heart. For this becomes your genuine expression of worship.
Stop imitating the ideals and opinions of the culture around you, but be inwardly transformed by the Holy Spirit through a total reformation of how you think. This will empower you to discern God's will as you live a beautiful life, satisfying and perfect in his eyes. [10]

Questions:

- What idols in our culture can you identify? How are you seeking to think and live differently?
- In making either leadership or day-to-day decisions, what steps could you take to ensure the good of the Christian Community, rather than what's just good for you?
- In what ways have you suffered because your faith has been distinctively different to the culture around you?"

---

[10] Rom 12:1-2 TPT

Chapter 7

A Shared Life

Early on in our marriage, Jenny and I decided that we wanted to have others living with us. It wasn't a particularly thought-through decision, but we had had it modelled to us by our church leaders, Dave and Rhi Day in Bristol. In fact I had lived with them for 6 months before we got married. I think it was simply the power of imitation at work, one of the greatest means of discipleship.

As our marriage approached, we decided we wanted to live as close to others in our church community as possible. God enabled us to get a flat that looked directly into Dave and Rhi's front room on the opposite side of the street. It seemed like God was making living in community very easy for us. We had experienced hospitality modelled to us and wanted to build that into our lifestyle. Our flat wasn't the most luxurious. It had two rooms divided into four. The instant gas heater nearly exploded every time someone ran the hot water, the so-called carpet in the front room had a serious infestation of ground-in chewing gum, and the bedroom was the size of two double beds. Nevertheless it was home, and we were where we wanted to be.

During our first year, we took in a friend who had been made homeless for a few weeks. He slept on our living room floor. It was our introduction to community living. The following year our landlord advised us that he was selling the building and we were to move out with the inducement of £100 to sweeten the pill. But community was still very high on our agenda and we didn't want to move away from Dave and Rhi. So we came up with a hair-brained scheme to buy the whole house.

Bear in mind that I was still studying as a medical student and Jenny had just graduated and was working in a shop. We had the princely income of £28 per week (it was 1976). However where there is God's will, there is God's way. We figured out that if we bought the property with another couple (our best man and bridesmaid), we could cobble together enough potential bits of income to build a reasonable case for a mortgage application. But we didn't have any deposit. Enter the first full-time lodger. Chris had £1000 saved and was willing to sink it into the house so we could raise the loan. A friendly building society manager (who just happened to be in the church) made the whole thing possible, and we became the proud joint owners of a Victorian semi. Eventually 3 couples lived in the house, in their own spaces, along with Chris, our lodger, who lived and ate with us.

We also had the get-away driver from a bank robbery gang who had just got out of prison, (they obviously didn't get away!) sleeping on the living room floor.

They were heady days of exploring community life. We went on eventually to own our own small terraced house, originally a two up, two down house, which had been extended into the roof space. At one time, as well as having our first two kids there, we also had three single girls (in one small bedroom), and in time a patient from the local psychiatric hospital where I was working at the time. At a later date we also had the get-away driver from a bank robbery gang who had just got out of prison, (they obviously didn't get away!) sleeping on the living room floor.

Since then we have had so many people live with us, that it almost certainly exceeds 100 people over the years. We've had people live with us in all of our 45 years of marriage. And it's been both a learning experience, and a wonderful experience. A challenging one, and a rich one. In the last couple of years, one of the most fascinating people to live with us was a young, rather lost Jamaican rapper, who was homeless before he moved in. He stayed about 6 weeks before heading back south.

Now, I am a card-carrying introvert, and people often ask me how I've survived. Well, the truth is I've not just survived, but thrived on the experience. Jenny and I often say it would be so boring just being the two of us (all kids left home some years ago). Yes, there are times when I need to go and find my own space, perhaps an hour with a good book in a coffee shop. But most of the time I love it.

I am aware that not everyone has space to have people live with them, and that there are times in the seasons of family life when it's not so easy to have others around. But it's amazing how you can find space when you want to, and how much our kids have enjoyed a rich variety of 'aunties and uncles' living with us. I know we made mistakes, but you can't do something you've never done before without figuring out some things the hard way!

Even if you live as a nuclear family, you can extend that family by having an open door and an open table. More about that in the next chapter. If you aren't having others through your house and round your table on a regular basis, you are missing out on one of the best parts of being in the body and becoming the Bride of Christ. And even during lockdown due to Covid-19, hospitality around the table had to be reinterpreted, but made possible by using conferencing applications and the phone! In fact, one of our highlights during lockdown was having a regular virtual meal with a couple who are dear to us. We ordered the same take-away and then set up our laptops on the table so we could see each other and chat as we ate. There was lots of hilarity. It worked remarkably well!

It is possible that we end up idolising the nuclear family

The converse is true, and it is possible that we end up idolising the nuclear family, protecting our privacy, independence, isolation, space and boundaries at all costs; all this at the expense of extended family. For most of history, for most cultures in the world, extended family was and is the norm. It's only in Western culture in the last 100 years that nuclear family, because of increasing prosperity, has become an option. In fact we should really think of extended family as the normal definition of the word family, and our nuclear family should be known as something like the reduced, underdeveloped, shrunken, wizened, or impoverished family. There's a challenge!

The aim of community living is not to benefit from the extra income or having built in baby-sitters, though both of those are certainly blessings, the reason for living like this (whether with people living in the house, or just regularly orbiting in and out) is to be able to experience a shared life. When we read of the early church we see just that. It breaks the power of individualism, of churlish self-centredness. It certainly stops you having unnecessary arguments with your spouse. It starts to model something of a kingdom community that is able to share and release resources for kingdom causes. We see the power of shared resources in Acts 2 and 4. Everything they owned was shared so that none had need.

Jenny and I have had people in our home for many reasons. Some just because they needed somewhere to live, others because they needed some emotional healing in a 'normal' family environment, but the most compelling reason has been when we have had the opportunity to disciple those under our roof. It's been the best way to get to grips with discipleship issues rapidly, and create a place of learning and accountability. However the reason we have most enjoyed having people is because of the fun it brings!

This Bride of Christ is a body of people who are deeply connected in their everyday life, in their struggles and in their joys. They are called out, set apart, connected with each other, and then sent out. The image of the body is a clear picture of what it means for each body part to be connected to another, and how none could function by themselves.[1]

There is nothing more fulfilling than figuring out how a community of God's people can find their God-given mission and purpose, and then each play their God-given part. When we all work together out of shared lives, the joy is great.

It was back in Jerusalem, 537 BC, 50 years after the temple had been destroyed by the Babylonian king Nebuchadnezzar. Some of the early group of Jews who had been allowed to return from captivity in exile to their homeland began to survey the desolation. They would have been a tight knit group with one thing in mind. Their mission, should they accept it – to rebuild the temple!

First the altar and then the foundations of the temple itself. Imagine the distraught Israelites when they first returned seeing their beloved glorious temple built by Solomon lying in ruins. Some said it couldn't be done. It took the prophesying of Haggai and Zechariah to encourage them and stir them to rebuild.

And then one day the foundations were complete. What joy! The book of Ezra records it like this:

When the builders completed the foundation of the Lord's Temple, the priests put on their robes and took their places

---

[1] I Cor 12

to blow their trumpets. And the Levites, descendants of Asaph, clashed their cymbals to praise the Lord, just as King David had prescribed. With praise and thanks, they sang this song to the Lord: "He is so good! His faithful love for Israel endures forever!"

Then all the people gave a great shout, praising the Lord because the foundation of the Lord's Temple had been laid. But many of the older priests, Levites, and other leaders who had seen the first Temple wept aloud when they saw the new Temple's foundation. The others, however, were shouting for joy. The joyful shouting and weeping mingled together in a loud noise that could be heard far in the distance.[2]

I hope you can catch the glorious chaotic excitement. They were full of shouts of joy and tears as well. The foundations were complete. They had finished Stage One of a great missional project, towards the restoration of God's purposes for Israel. Similar joy was evident when the temple was complete. They had pulled together and managed what many thought was impossible. There was a whole lot of celebrating and eating together going on.

Then they celebrated the Festival of Unleavened Bread for seven days. There was great joy throughout the land because the Lord had caused the king of Assyria to be favourable to them, so that he helped them to rebuild the Temple of God, the God of Israel.[3]

---

[2] Ezra 3:10-13 NLT
[3] Ezra 6:22 NLT

God has called us to live as a family on mission, a people with purpose, a community with a cause. We were not designed to live alone, in our castle-like homes. We were called to live in community. We are called to be hospitable, it's time to let down the drawbridge. And even if we can't or don't have people living with us, we can all make our home a place where others regularly come to eat and be together.

God has called us to live as a family on mission, a people with purpose, a community with a cause.

We are called to do this not for expediency or for its own sake. There is always a cost to living a shared life in community. So we don't do it with idealistic rose-tinted spectacles, imagining that it will all be sweetness and light all of the time. If we live in community for community's sake it will not last for long. It will start to unravel sooner or later. We do it because it is good for us, because it reflects the nature of the Godhead, and because it creates resources for a shared mission in the world around us. There is a cost, but it's worth it.

Shared living also gives the best opportunities for discipleship. There is nothing like doing the chores together to discover where people need help in their personal development. Praying together regularly provides a backdrop to other spiritual conversations. And more structured times of input, with accountability, are easy to arrange. Our lives of course are on display – how we treat our family, how we use our spare time, how we respond to set backs and frustration, how we handle our finances etc. And this is part of the challenge. But what a great opportunity to disciple through the power of imitation.

One young man who lived with us for a year before getting married didn't at the time seem to be particularly keen to learn from us, but years later admitted that, having come from a dysfunctional family, learnt everything he knew about marriage from that year living with us. Thankfully he has a great marriage!

The Greek word for hospitality is *'philoxenia'*. It is the opposite of our modern word xenophobia, which means the fear of or hatred of strangers. Philoxenia means the love of the stranger. Scripture is clear that it's something we can and should all embrace.

When God's people are in need, be ready to help them. Always be eager to practice hospitality.[4]

Most important of all, continue to show deep love for each other, for love covers a multitude of sins. Cheerfully share your home with those who need a meal or a place to stay.[5]

'The problem with the world is that we draw the circle of our family too small'.

Mother Teresa said 'the problem with the world is that we draw the circle of our family too small'. I like that. Our family is God's answer to loneliness. The psalmist said that 'God places the solitary in families.'[6] At the very beginning God said that it wasn't good for man to be alone.[7] Family is his idea. He modelled it first. He created it. He invites us to be his family by practicing family, and offering family to those on the edge.

It's an indictment of our present culture in the UK that we have needed to appoint a government minister for loneliness! And the rise in mental health issues is in some significant

---

4 Rom 12:13 NLT
5 1 Peter 4:8-9 NLT
6 Ps 68:6 AMPC
7 Gen 2:18

measure due to family breakdown and social isolation. The world is crying out for healthy families. Jesus said we are the salt of the earth, bringing flavour and preservation to our culture. He also said that we are the light of the world, pointing to a 'better way', and telling a better story.[8] Living in God's design for family, in shared life, also points others to the perfect Father and perfect family of Father, Son and Holy Spirit.

Family of course doesn't mean just married couples with children. There are all types of families, including households that are made up of singles, single parents, and other types of communal expressions. It's the quality of the shared life that counts, not the structure of those who are sharing it.

It's time to open our homes, to practice hospitality, to share our lives with one another. It's a hallmark of the Bride, of the church that Jesus died for and is coming back for.

Questions:

- What experience have you had of 'shared life', and what was it like?
- What most challenges you about the idea or practice of living a 'shared life'?
- How do you think you could make the 'circle of your family' a little bigger?

---

[8] Matt 5:13-16

Chapter 8

A Shared Table

A natural follow-on from a shared life is a shared table. In fact I think it's fair to say that the shared table is at the heart of a shared life.

Author Tim Chester says that Jesus spent one third of his time either on his way to a meal, at a meal, or on his way from a meal.[1] He inaugurated his new covenant with a meal. It is what we know as the Last Supper, but the first of the church's regular shared meals where we remember his death and resurrection. He invites us as his Bride to a celebratory wedding feast.[2] The disciples broke bread from house to house, and took their meals together with glad and sincere hearts.[3] Do you get the idea? Eating together is big in God's mind!

I love the fact that there are three 'the Son of Man came...' scriptures in the gospels.

The first is 'the Son of Man came not to be served but to serve and give his life as a ransom for many'.[4]

---

[1] A Meal With Jesus: Discovering Grace, Community And Mission Around The Table. Tim Chester. IVP
[2] Rev 19:6-9
[3] Acts 2:46
[4] Matt 20:28, Mark 10:45

The second is 'the Son of Man came to seek and save the lost.'[5]

So far, so good. All pretty weighty matters you might think. The third is a bit of a surprise. A bit of a curve ball.

'The Son of Man came eating and drinking...'[6]

Wow, wasn't expecting that! And it begins to highlight the importance of the shared table. I believe the shared meal was one of Jesus' key strategies for both evangelism and discipleship.

Time for a little Greek again. There are two words that are often translated joy in the New Testament. The first and most common is 'chara', for example, 'consider it all joy (chara)... when you encounter various trials.'[7] In its various forms it occurs 59 times in the New Testament. There is another more curious, more intriguing, little known and wonderful word that appears in four passages. It is the word 'agalliasis'.

Let's check out where we find it in the New Testament.

It occurs in the gospels when Mary meets Elizabeth. John the Baptist, who is probably about 6 months' developed in Elizabeth's womb, 'leaps for joy' in acknowledgement that he has encountered Jesus, just conceived, in Mary's womb.[8] Joy here, is the word 'agalliasis'.

---

[5] Lk 19:10
[6] Lk 7:34
[7] Jas 1:2 NASB
[8] Lk 1:44

In the book of Hebrews the writer, quoting Isaiah 61:3, describes Jesus as being 'set above [his] companions by being anointed with the oil of joy' (*agalliasis*).[9]

In the book of Jude we read that God will 'keep you from stumbling and make you stand in the presence of his glory, blameless with great joy (*agalliasis*).'[10] What a great moment when the Bride will stand before the Bridegroom, at the moment when they are finally united and made one for all eternity. Great joy!

Note that these examples are all moments when Jesus is revealed – to John the Baptist in the womb, in the messianic scriptures as the anointed one, and finally when we meet him face to face in the day of his coming. It's all about Jesus. In fact, the word '*agalliasis*' is really best translated as 'extreme joy'. It's an altogether different type and level of joy compared with '*chara*'.

So where do you think the fourth use of the word comes?

This is where the fun begins. It occurs in the verse we have already quoted from Acts 2.

They worshipped together at the Temple each day, met in homes for the Lord's Supper, and shared their meals with great joy and generosity.[11]

Yes, it's the word '*agalliasis*'. No ordinary joy as the disciples shared their meals together. It was the extreme joy, the moment when Jesus is revealed at the shared table. It included, but was not limited to, the breaking of bread. This should be no surprise when we remember that Jesus

---

[9] Heb 1:9
[10] Jude 1:24 NASB
[11] Acts 2:46 NLT

revealed himself to the two disciples on the road to Emmaus in the breaking of bread.

As they sat down to eat, he took the bread and blessed it. Then he broke it and gave it to them. Suddenly, their eyes were opened, and they recognized him. And at that moment he disappeared! They said to each other, "Didn't our hearts burn within us as he talked with us on the road and explained the Scriptures to us?"[12]

Yes, it was in the shared meal that Jesus was revealed to them. Their hearts 'burned within them'. I like to think they had a little touch of the '*agalliasis*'. The extreme joy of his presence.

You see, sharing our table is not just a practical way of spending time together, blessing others, and including them in our family life, but it also has the potential to be a moment when Jesus is revealed as the unseen guest at the meal table, when our hearts burn within us and we are filled with extreme joy. Does that sound good? It does to me!

In our household we make it a priority to share our meal table, not only with those who live with us, but with others too. Those who love Jesus and those who don't know him yet. And we get a glimpse of Jesus, a touch of that extreme joy from time to time. It is precious.

It's good to break bread round the table. It doesn't need to be an authorised communion service requiring the presence of an ordained priest (thankfully). It is simply disciples sharing a meal together, and in the middle of that meal, breaking and sharing bread, and sharing in a cup of wine or grape juice, remembering that he is with us. The Bridegroom is present. We eat in anticipation of the day when we will be united, Bride

---

[12] Lk 24:30-32 NLT

with Bridegroom. As the Apostle Paul put it when writing to the Corinthian church, we share this bread and wine 'announcing the Lord's death until he comes again'.[13]

What greater way could there be to be reminded constantly of that great wedding day than at the meal table, sharing in bread and wine?

I have a suspicion that we have made breaking bread far too religious. As much as anything else it was a normal part of a Jewish meal at the time of Jesus, and still is for many cultures in the world today. It was the moment when the bread got shared out. The blessing of it would have been similar to our giving thanks before a meal time. It was all very normal.

We have a little ritual in our home. I call it the Harding communion toast. It's a simple way to keep this reality present in our minds, even when we are just having a glass of wine. When the glasses are all filled, one of us announces the toast by raising their glass and saying 'to the King.' The others respond with 'until he comes'. It is a simple way of staying engaged with a future reality, sharing in the cup which he lifted at the last supper, and will not take again till he comes again in his Father's kingdom.[14]

I hope you have a new appreciation of the incredible value of a shared table. I am very aware when young children are present it won't always seem like these are profound moments of revelation, more like pressured moments of frustration. But let's look for the presence of Jesus with our friends around the shared table even in these crazy chaotic moments of very normal family life.

---

[13] 1 Cor 11:26 NLT
[14] Matt 26:29

And let's be clear, we are not all going to be a Jamie Oliver or Thomas Keller, but we can all throw some spuds in the oven, heat some baked beans and grate some cheese to go over the top. We can all put a frozen pizza in the oven and serve it with some garlic bread (even I can do that!). It doesn't have to be cordon bleu. It just needs to be shared with love.

Questions:

- If you've ever had a moment when it felt like Jesus was revealing himself at the table, what happened?
- How would you feel about opening up your table to others outside the immediate family? How could you talk about this with others you live with?
- How could you build in a simple rhythm of sharing your meal table with others?

Part 3 – Invincible Army

A book about a Bride seems incongruous with a section on being an invincible army. However nothing could be further from the truth. As we consider the events of the end times (more of this later), we see in the book of Revelation, battle after battle.

This beautiful glorious Bride comes not neatly packaged from the bridal outfitters, but with the smell of smoke from the battlefield. Her scars will make her all the more beautiful to her Bridegroom, the Captain of the Lord of Hosts – the Lord of Lords, and the King of Kings.[1] The Bridegroom himself comes from the final battle to greet his Bride.[2]

The battlefields of this age are the training for reigning in a future age.[3]

The Apostle John writes,

And they sang a new song with these words: "You are worthy to take the scroll and break its seals and open it. For you were slaughtered, and your blood has ransomed people for God from every tribe and language and people and nation.

---

[1] Rev 19:11-19
[2] Rev 21:2-3
[3] Read more about this idea in Paul E Billheimer's book 'Destined for the Throne'. Bethany House Publishers

And you have caused them to become a Kingdom of priests for our God. And they will reign on the earth."[4]

The ultimate victory has of course already been won at the cross and through the resurrection of Jesus.[5] But we are called, as his invincible army, to enforce that victory in the time we are in now, between the death blow being struck by Christ at his first coming, and the final destruction of Satan and his demons at the end of time at Christ's second coming.[6]

The Bride will be glorious and beautiful, not because she has avoided the battle, but precisely because she has embraced it.

So what does this look like?

—————————————

[4] Rev 5:9-10 NLT
[5] Col 2:13-15, Heb 2:14-15
[6] Rev 20:10

Chapter 9

The Battle is Real

I quote this story from my book 'Living on the Frontline: A beginner's guide to spiritual warfare'[1]:

'It was a relatively ordinary Sunday afternoon in November 1997 when the phone rang. I picked it up and heard my wife Jenny's voice for a brief second. Then all I could hear was the sound of emergency vehicles in the background before the call cut out – In a moment like that, every possible scenario goes through your mind. All I knew was that something awful had happened and Jenny was trying to contact me.

I frantically tried to contact her but was unable to do so. I began the task of ringing the police to see if there had been an accident. Eventually, I was put through to someone who informed me that yes, Mrs Harding had been involved in an accident. They didn't know how serious it was, but thought they were on their way to Arrowe Park Hospital on the Wirral.

A week earlier, Jenny and I had been in Pensacola witnessing first-hand the revival scenes at Brownsville Church. We had returned to the UK extremely excited and

---

[1] Living on the Front Line: A beginner's guide to spiritual warfare. Nic Harding. Republished by Create Space Independent Publishing Platform, 2017

envisioned as to the impact this could have on our own church.

On our return to Liverpool, we shared in the Sunday morning meeting. There was an amazing response from people and we had the opportunity to pray with many. It was on this same day that Jenny decided to go to the Ellesmere Port retail outlet with our two youngest daughters, aged 13 and 14, and one of their friends.

As I raced to the hospital, I was filled with a strange calm (which can only have been the peace of God), but also a sense of apprehension as to what I would find. On arrival, I discovered that the car had been written-off, that Jenny and two of the girls had suffered whiplash and some bruising, but that one of my daughters was more seriously injured. X-rays eventually revealed that she had broken her spine and, because the fracture was right through one of the vertebrae, it was a potentially very serious situation where any movement of the bone could have caused paralysis.

After three weeks in hospital, a major spinal operation, and a further operation to remove some damaged bowel, she finally came out of hospital sporting a full (but removable) body cast, and made her way towards total recovery. Thankfully, today she is able to do everything she wants to do and, apart from the occasional backache or muscle spasm, is symptom-free. (One small perk for her was that she did get to travel business class when she had to fly abroad for work. The guys who travelled with her, twice her size, were cooped up in economy quietly fuming!)

You are probably wondering what all this has got to do with the spiritual battle. Well, to understand the situation you need to know what was happening on a different continent at the same time…

In the hours building up to the accident, Dave Connolly (my wonderful co-pastor) was in Richmond, Virginia, in the United States. During the night, he had a horrific nightmare in which he found himself battling with dark, demonic objects who were trying to attack Jenny, our two youngest daughters and a third girl he didn't recognise. After wrestling for what seemed like an eternity, he managed to subdue the opponents and they slunk off, but not before a final shot of some sort went over Dave's head. He was unable to stop it.

He woke up feeling exhausted but, sensing the dream was significant, wrote it down immediately. He went back to sleep and twice more had the same dream with the same experience. He felt exhausted by the battle. When he woke in the morning and got to the church where he was preaching, he shared it with the pastor there. The pastor felt it was a warning sign, and decided that they should pray for our family. So there and then the whole church was asked to intercede for our family's protection, particularly for Jenny and the girls.

We can't be sure about the exact timings, but it seems likely that this prayer was taking place just moments before the accident happened. Minutes before the accident, Jenny had also suddenly felt prompted to make sure the girls in the back were wearing their seatbelts. Coincidence? I don't think so. I believe this was a severe attack from the enemy seeking to wipe out my family, probably in response to the new levels of faith and anointing we'd recently received, and were seeking to pass on to the church. At any rate, it is the most serious attack our family has ever experienced.

The wonderful thing was that even though God allowed us to go through this experience, he was not standing back passively. He was working actively by sending a warning (through Dave) that the enemy was at work, and by engaging other Christians to intercede for us. I believe that without such interventions, one or more of my family would have undoubtedly been killed on that day.

What had happened was that an elderly couple had just returned from Canada and were badly jetlagged. They were driving along the A41, a section of dual carriageway without a central reservation on the Wirral. The wife (who was the passenger) dozed off first and was eventually followed by her husband, who fell asleep over the wheel due to his tiredness and jetlag. Their car swerved across the central reservation and straight into our oncoming car. There was no warning, no way the accident could have been avoided, and probably a total collision speed of around 80 miles per hour. The car was a complete write-off, with the front end totally caved in – what a miraculous escape!

> We need to be ready, not just to repel the enemy's attacks, but to take the battle to his gates and plunder his territory.

Thank God for his protection and for others' sensitivity to the Holy Spirit's warnings. I say all this not to frighten you, but to emphasise the reality of the spiritual battle in which we live and with which we must engage. We cannot bury our heads in the sand. As it says in the Apostle Peter's first letter "Be self-controlled and alert. Your enemy the devil prowls around like a roaring lion looking for someone to devour."[2] We need to be ready, not just to repel the enemy's attacks, but to take the battle to his gates and plunder his territory.

Scripture is clear. The Apostle Paul says 'endure suffering along with me, as a good soldier of Christ Jesus. Soldiers

---

[2] 1 Pet 5:8

don't get tied up in the affairs of civilian life, for then they cannot please the officer who enlisted them.'[3]

The battle is real, but the outcome is not in doubt. The Apostle John in his Revelation tells us 'And they overcame him because of the blood of the Lamb and because of the word of their testimony, and they did not love their life even when faced with death.'[4]

The churches of Revelation chapters 2 and 3 are all issued with the challenge, 'to him who overcomes...' We will all have our battles. It's part of the qualification for being the Bride. But in every battle there are casualties, losses, injuries and setbacks. So we are to embrace suffering as good soldiers, equip ourselves so we are ready to fight, and know whom our squad, platoon, company and battalion are. We are going to need them.

Questions:

- What experiences of this spiritual battle have you had?
- How do you feel about being a part of a military Bride?
- Who are your squad (a group of between 6-12 people), and platoon (20-50 people), the people God has called you to live, work and fight alongside?

---

[3] 2 Tim 2:3-4   NLT
[4] Rev 12:11 NASB

Chapter 10

Unity and Authority

An army that is to be invincible must understand both the power of unity, and the importance of authority.

Unity
We've looked at the Bride as radical community. That word *community* is of course made up of two parts, *com + unity*, literally 'with unity'.

No army succeeds when it is disunited, when women and men are all doing their own thing, choosing their own strategy, their own timing and their own buddies for their enterprises. Sadly, this is rampant in today's church, and is one of the manifestations of the radical individualism of our culture. We have lost the priority of unity, other than in a vaguely sentimental sense, or from a purely theological perspective. We fail to work through our differences so that we can move as one. The Apostle Paul says that we are to be 'united in spirit, intent on one purpose'.[1] Our unity must make a difference to our daily lives.

The enemy knows that if he can divide us he can defeat us in that particular battle. Our unity is powerful. Jesus said that

---

[1] Phil 2:2 NASB

our prayers are amplified and made more potent by our unity.[2]

Unity is a gift received from the Holy Spirit when we are born again. Our starting state is the unity that we have from him. However, that unity has to be maintained. The Apostle Paul writing to the church in Ephesus says,

...[be] diligent to preserve the unity of the Spirit in the bond of peace.[3]

Note the word *diligent*. It requires effort and persistence. I know that every time I mess up in a relationship, the temptation is to do nothing. I know that it will be painful to go back and try to repair the unity with that sister or brother. I remember getting a bit hot under the collar during a moment when I was preaching. One of the children was making a lot of noise and disturbing everyone around them. They were certainly disturbing me. I made a rather unkind request for the child to be taken out of the room. Later that day I realised I had deeply upset the mum who was doing her best with a child that was not easy to manage. I rang them up and apologised. It wasn't easy. I felt foolish and humbled. But the result was so worth it. I've had a good relationship with that lovely mum ever since.

> *Maintaining unity requires constant diligence.*

Maintaining unity requires constant diligence. It needs a willingness to be the first to apologise. It is built on humility. We must see the situation from the other's point of view. It reflects the ministry of reconciliation that God entrusts to each of us.[4] If we can't be reconciled

---

[2] Matt 18:19-20
[3] Eph 4:3 NASB
[4] 2 Cor 5:19

with each other, how can we be agents of reconciliation, helping others be reconciled to God?

Offence is the usual culprit in relational breakdown. Taking offence will build a fence (sorry about the pun). How do we deal with offence? There are a number of options.

Firstly, just get over it! We take offence far too quickly over the smallest of things. 'You didn't say hello to me when you walked in the room'; 'you didn't thank me for my gift'; 'you didn't invite me to the pub with the others'; or 'you looked at me all wrong'. Come on, we need to just let the small stuff go, it is rare that offence was intended.

Secondly, we go to the person involved. Whether we are the offended one, or the one who has become aware of another who has taken offence with us (like me with the mum I offended). Jesus is clear, 'Go to them'.[5] It's not good enough to think, 'Well, they are offended with me, it's up to them to come and sort it out, it's not my problem'. We are as guilty of the disunity as they are.

Thirdly, Jesus says if all else fails, we are to take another with us to help resolve the issue.[6] Sometimes we get stuck in an entrenched view of the situation, only able to see it from our perspective. There are always two points of view, and both are valid. A third party is sometimes able to help both parties see the other's point of view.

There is often more heat than light in these situations and we can usually benefit from trying to find a place of peace before diving in to resolve a dispute. If the conflict has come in the workplace, there are probably procedures to follow to deal

---

[5] Matt 18:15
[6] Matt 18:16-17

with that, but in everyday life and especially in church life, we can be guided by Jesus' advice.

Forgiveness of course is key. It is costly to let another person off the hook for the things we think they have done or said wrong. But without forgiveness there can be no reconciliation. And without reconciliation there can be no unity. Jesus paid the price for our forgiveness on the cross. The price we pay is minimal by comparison.

The Bride will be united in the day of Jesus' return. It's pretty hard to imagine how that will work, with so many divisions and differences in the body of Christ. But the more we relate to each other in humility, teachability and love, the more unity we will find, even if we don't agree on every point of doctrine or practice. We can honour one another and love the different expressions of the body of Christ without competition, comparison or condemnation.

In the film 'The Two Popes', Pope Benedict is played by Anthony Hopkins, and his successor Pope Francis is played by Jonathan Pryce. The film charts the relationship between the two men from the announcement of Pope Benedict's appointment. Pope Francis is then Cardinal Bergoglio in Argentina. They are two completely different animals. Benedict is the aloof academic, conservative, preserver of the status quo, and Bergoglio is the progressive, man of the people, rule-breaking radical. Benedict relishes his rise to power, Bergoglio wants no place in the power structuroo, and definitely doesn't want to be Pope.

As the film progresses Bergoglio is frustrated with the lack of change in the church and travels to Rome to hand in his resignation as Cardinal. He and Benedict clash at so many levels, theologically, socially, in leadership style, and in their view of the future. The exchanges are heated and real animosity is shown. But as the relationship progresses over the coming days, a strange thing happens and is very moving. They learn to hear each other, they humble themselves before each other, and they develop a profound appreciation for the other. It's a great example of very different followers of Jesus being reconciled and finding common ground.

The rest as they say is history. Benedict stands down and Bergoglio becomes Pope Francis. The final scene is of the two of them sharing a drink together, laughing with each other, watching the 2014 World Cup final between Argentina and Germany, their two nations of origin. It is very funny and moving.

If this bears any relation to the truth, it is a great example of what can happen when we learn to humble ourselves, become learners more than experts and discover the Christ who is in the other.

When Paul writes to the church in Philippi, he exhorts them to be 'united in spirit, intent on one purpose'. [7] Our unity is not just about the absence of conflict, but also the presence of shared purpose.

> *Our unity is not just about the absence of conflict, but also the presence of shared purpose.*

Unity grows as we engage with a shared sense of what God is calling us to do together. This is really important in marriages, in missional communities, and as whole churches. Whilst that clarity around purpose can evolve over time, it must be pursued just as relational unity must be pursued.

God's purpose for the church is not only to become his Bride in heaven for all eternity, but while on earth, that purpose is

---

[7] Phil 2:2 NASB

expressed in the mission in which he has called us to share. The God who came to earth as a man, shared fully in our humanity, called and trained those who followed him, and suffered as much as any human being when crucified for each of us. This same man invites us into his mission. The mission is to represent him to a broken world, reconciling women and men to the Father, proclaiming and demonstrating the good news of the kingdom in every aspect of our lives, and inviting others into that kingdom to become part of his growing family, the maturing Bride of Jesus.

What does that shared purpose look like for you in the context of Jesus' mission to mankind? The two clarifying questions you need to ask are as follows.
- To whom are you called?
- With whom are you called?

These two questions are central to discovering the purpose in our unity. We are all called to reach others with the good news of his kingdom; we just need to figure out to whom or to where. Then we need to know who our team are, those who will be our squad or platoon, to use the military analogy. There is more about the nuts and bolts of how we do this in my book 'Reimagine Church'.[8]

In our Liverpool City Region in the UK, we have a network of churches under the banner of 'Together for the Harvest'.[9] Our strap line is 'reaching every man, woman and child with the gospel', and we use the Philippians 2:2 scripture about 'being united in Spirit, intent on one purpose' as a guiding principle.

---

[8] Reimagine Church, Nic Harding, Missio Publishing, especially the 7Ps of finding, defining, refining your missional purpose in Chapter 8
[9] www.tfh.org.uk

Over the years, hundreds of churches have worked together on different projects. When we first arrived in the city in 1991 it was a very different church scene from today. There had been a lot of disunity, church splits, isolation and competition. As the missional message started to take hold in the 90s, the church started to come together – for the harvest.

This is replicated all over the UK, with unity movements in over 130 towns and cities registered with Gather, the national network of unity movements.[10]

Unity must happen not only within churches, but also between churches. It's interesting that the only kind of church recognised in the New Testament is the church in the house and the church in the city. If we are to truly become the BRIDE of Christ we have to put away our rivalries, our non-essential doctrinal differences, our insecurities, and our need to prove that we have the biggest or best church in the city.

This will be evidenced by bonds of friendship and prayer between pastors, shared resources and projects between churches (social, evangelistic and church planting projects), common vision to see every man, woman and child reached, and our cities transformed by the gospel. This will delight the heart of God, help to complete the great commission in our cities, and prepare us for the return of the Bridegroom.

As I write this I'm preparing to meet with half a dozen other church leaders in Liverpool, to share lunch and pray with each other. This group has been together in various combinations for over 15 years. It supported me through some of my darkest times in church leadership. It has been a lifeline for many of us. It is a place where we can be rooting for each other, laugh together, share our challenges, pray for one another, and encourage each other to keep going. It's a great expression of the unity of the body citywide.

---

[10] www.gather.global

Authority

In the military context, unity is also built through clear authority structures and the direction for the mission that is given through them. And here the analogy breaks down. In the military, authority is very top-down, hierarchical and often controlling. In some senses, it has to be in that context. We need a clear understanding of how authority operates in God's invincible army, the church.

We know that God has placed authority in the world as well as the church. I find it interesting that the second half of the book of Ephesians deals with a variety of authority contexts, namely church (along with teaching on maintaining unity)[11], marriage [12], family life [13], and the workplace. [14] It is no coincidence that these all precede the great section on spiritual warfare. [15] How important that we engage in the battles with a full appreciation of God's provision of authority.

Authority within the church is very different from that top-down style of the military. It is bottom up, it is servant-hearted, it is given not taken, it is to protect and release, not to exploit and control, and it is self-effacing not self-promoting. Christ himself inaugurated this style of leadership. As is often said, he is the servant king.

> Authority is primarily worked out is through mutual submission to the gifts and callings on each person.

The way in which authority is primarily worked out is through mutual submission to the gifts

---

[11] Eph 4
[12] Eph 5:21-33
[13] Eph 6:1-4
[14] Eph 6:5-9
[15] Eph 6:10-20

and callings on each person. Ephesians 4 talks about the ministry gifts of apostle, prophet, evangelist, shepherd and teacher[16], but there are many other gifts we do well to acknowledge and submit to.[17] This is not the authority of status or position, but of gift and calling.

It's a little like the authority of the plumber or surgeon. I'm stupid not to submit to them if I need to fix a leaking water pipe, or a diseased organ.

There is also the authority of the elders. These are those who are called to watch over the flock, to guard it and protect it from the 'wild beasts', from Satan's schemes. Here the authority is not over the people, but is authority to serve the people. It is however over the demonic realm, in pursuit of the church's protection and deliverance from the evil one.

Direction is given through the gifts and ministries to the body. Protection is given through the elders (or the equivalent in that church's context), or more generally through the spiritual mothers and fathers in the church family. Paul appealed to the Corinthian church as a spiritual father.[18] He had planted the church in Corinth and spent 18 months growing and establishing the work. He had every right to appeal to them from his position of leadership, but instead wrote to them as a spiritual father. This is the authority of an elder, literally someone who is older – older in the faith, and usually but not always older in age. An elder's authority is not primarily positional, but stems from their recognised spiritual maturity and wisdom.

So we gladly submit ourselves to such servant authority. We would be wary to do so if those exercising the authority

---

[16] Eph 4:11-13
[17] Rom 12:4-13, I Cor 12:1-11, 27-31
[18] 1 Cor 4:15

seemed to have a different motive, that of control, domination or exploitation. If we encounter such an aberration of God's gift of authority to the church, we are probably in the wrong church.

Having said all of that, authority is as important in the church as in the military, it just looks very different. We will not fulfil our potential as an invincible army without both pursuing unity, and seeking out God's authority. Both are for our blessing.

Where God has placed his authority, whether through gift and ministry, or through the presence of spiritual mothers and fathers, we do well to gladly submit to that authority and benefit from the blessing that it is to us.

Questions:

- Where have you found maintaining unity most challenging?
- Whom might you need to forgive or go to for reconciliation?
- What helpful expressions of authority can you identify in your local church that you can gladly submit to? Which ones are less helpful and why?

Chapter 11

Trained and Equipped

An invincible army needs to be both trained and equipped for the battle. I've written quite a bit on personal equipping through identity and prayer, and on training for communities on mission in 'Reimagine Church'[1] and 'Living on the Frontline'[2], so I won't repeat all

Most of us are neither ready to protect ourselves, nor to take the battle to the enemy's gates

of that here. Suffice it to say, most of us are neither ready to protect ourselves, nor to take the battle to the enemy's gates.[3]

The famous passage in Ephesians[4] on spiritual warfare begins with a description of the armour of God – the belt of truth, the breastplate of righteousness, the readiness or preparation of the gospel of peace, the shield of faith, the helmet of salvation, and the sword of the Spirit.

---

[1] Reimagine Church, Nic Harding, Missio Publishing
[2] Living on the Frontline: a beginners guide to spiritual warfare, Republished by Create Space Independent Publishing Platform, 2017
[3] Matt 16:18
[4] Eph 6:13-17

Did you notice that five of the six pieces of armour are defensive? This should wake us up to the fact that we need to know how to defend ourselves every moment of every day. The devil is like a roaring lion seeking whom he may devour, he is the accuser and deceiver[5], he is the tempter[6], and he has schemes to entrap us.[7]

So, learning to live in the good of the armour, the lifestyle of the trained and equipped soldier is vital, so that we aren't caught unawares and knocked out of the battle. There are far too many casualties on the battlefield for us to feel blasé about the enemy's attacks. Jesus even teaches his disciples to pray 'lead us not into temptation, but deliver us from the evil one'[8], as part of his key teaching on prayer.

Some of the main blockages to getting trained are the lack of a teachable heart, an accountable lifestyle, and the presence of a mentor, coach or spiritual parent. Finding the right person is crucial to being trained, otherwise we are doomed to learn everything the hard way, by our mistakes. While our failures and mistakes are a rich source of learning, I'd rather avoid the unnecessary ones.

Ideally we can find someone to speak into our lives, and to whom we can make ourselves accountable within our small group or missional community. Those we are sharing life with are the ones most likely to be looking out for us and able to spot the early signs of us getting ourselves into trouble. This kind of spiritual family should operate like the natural family, with spiritual mums and dads who are looking out for us and helping us grow in courage and confidence in the battle. Peer accountability can work fine, but to really be equipped for the

---

[5] Rev 12:9-10 NASB
[6] Matt 4:1, 1 Cor 7:5
[7] 2 Cor 2:11
[8] Matt 6:13

battle we need someone who has a few battle scars themselves.

For all my Christian life I have sought out mentors and those I can be accountable to. I value those people who have provided that in the past and still do today.

The one piece of armour that is clearly offensive, as opposed to defensive, is the sword of the Spirit, the word of God. We need to pay particular attention to our spiritual disciplines in the word. Jesus used the word to defeat the enemy in the wilderness. Time and time again when tempted by Satan he replies with 'it is written...'.[9]

The word of God is primarily the written word of God in the Bible, but when the Apostle Paul writes to Timothy, he encourages him to make use of prophetic words he has received to fight his battles. When tested and applied appropriately, they are another dimension of the sword of the Spirit, which is the word of God.

So Timothy, my son, I am entrusting you with this responsibility, in keeping with the very first prophecies that were spoken over your life, and are now in the process of fulfilment in this great work of ministry... With this encouragement use your prophecies as weapons as you wage spiritual warfare by faith and with a clean conscience...[10]

I have kept a record of significant prophetic words that I have received over the years. They are a great source, not only of encouragement, but also in providing faith and fuel for the battles.

---

[9] Lk 4:4
[10] 1 Tim 1:18-19 TPT

The word of God can be used in prayer. When we quote scriptural truths and promises they release faith and power over the powers of darkness. If we are facing a particular battle we can find a truth or promise and claim its benefits, while rebuking the enemy's attempt to tempt us, discourage us, or knock us off course.

The Apostle James says:

So humble yourselves before God. Resist the devil, and he will flee from you. Come close to God, and God will come close to you. Wash your hands, you sinners; purify your hearts, for your loyalty is divided between God and the world. [11]

In the context of humbling ourselves, drawing close to God, purifying our hearts, and dealing with worldly compromise we are called to resist the devil. Let's do so using the word of God just like Jesus did. So being prepared requires us not only having some key scriptures to quote but also to be living a lifestyle where the enemy has no grounds for accusation.

> We are called to resist the devil

The passage on the armour of God leads straight into what many consider to be two of the most powerful offensive weapons for the battle. If the Bride is going to be this invincible army, then it needs to grow in both of these. They are prayer and the preaching of the gospel. The Apostle Paul concludes this passage on spiritual warfare saying,

And pray in the Spirit on all occasions with all kinds of prayers and requests. With this in mind, be alert and always keep on praying for all the Lord's people. Pray also for me, that whenever I speak, words may be given me so that I will

---

[11] Jas 4:7-8 NLT

fearlessly make known the mystery of the gospel, for which I am an ambassador in chains. Pray that I may declare it fearlessly, as I should.[12]

The sword of the Spirit that is the word of God is both tested prophetic words and the written word of God, but it is also the gospel proclaimed. There is nothing that Satan hates more than when we boldly declare the good news about Jesus and his kingdom. Prayer and the proclamation of the gospel are the pinnacle of this passage on spiritual warfare.

Questions:

- Are you able to identify a spiritual mother or father, a mentor or coach, someone to whom you can be accountable, who speaks into your life? If so, how could you develop that relationship to be more effective in equipping you? If not, how could you find such a person?
- What sort of spiritual battles are you facing and in what ways would you say you are equipped with God's word for the battle?

---

[12] Eph 6:18-20

Chapter 12

Perseverance and Persecution

There are five words that don't make it onto many sermon series these days. I call them the 5Ss. They are:
- Service
- Submission
- Surrender
- Sacrifice
- Suffering

Not everyone's favourite topics!

But there is a sense in which all are required if we are going to be that invincible army, that military Bride that stands with the warrior Bridegroom.

Service
Jesus made it clear to his disciples that they were to emulate him, the one who was called 'not to be served but to serve and give his life as a ransom for many'.[1]

The history of the early church is one of serving communities, serving the poor and the suffering, usually at their own expense, and sometimes at the expense of their own lives.

---

[1] Matt 20:28

One of the early church fathers, Tertullian, said this (AD197): 'These gifts are . . . not spent on feasts, and drinking-bouts, and eating-houses, but to support and bury poor people, to supply the wants of boys and girls destitute of means and parents, and of old persons confined now to the house; such, too, as have suffered shipwreck; and if there happen to be any in the mines or banished to the islands or shut up in the prisons, for nothing but their fidelity to the cause of God's Church, they become the nurslings of their confession'.[2]

The church is always at its best when it is serving. As Archbishop William Temple[3] said 'The Church is the only institution that exists primarily for the benefit of those who are not its members.'[4]

Submission
Our submission is crucial both in our relationship to Jesus as Lord, but also in our seeking out his gift of authority to us in the church, as described previously. We are also to have an attitude of mutual submission to one another.[5]

Surrender
Surrendering to God takes this a step further when we recognise that everything we have is his – our time, our energy, our gifts, our material possession, our relationships, our affections and our influence. As we surrender them all to him, we discover that he can make far better use of all these God-given resources than we can by ourselves.

---

[2] The Apology of Tertullian
[3] Archbishop William Temple was Archbishop of Canterbury from 1942-1944
[4] From William Temple's book 'Christianity and the Social Order'
[5] Eph 5:21

Surrender (and Sacrifice, below) is rooted in the knowledge that we are called into a crucified life. We have been crucified with Christ and it is no longer us who live, but Christ who lives in us.[6] That's why the Apostle Paul also says that we are to consider ourselves dead to sin but

This crucified life is a daily choice. It is both painful and wonderfully liberating.

alive to God in Christ.[7] This crucified life is a daily choice. It is both painful and wonderfully liberating. The love of comfort will always be beckoning us off the cross, but the freedom and life of God is found in this crucified life. We say with Jesus, 'not my will but yours be done.'[8]

Sacrifice

Sacrifice is the natural outcome from believing something to be of greater value than our own comfort or convenience. These could be small sacrifices of time or money, or much bigger ones like careers, homes, or even family. The Apostle Peter commented to Jesus that the disciples had left everything to follow him. Jesus' reply is this,

"Truly I tell you, there is no one who has left house or brothers or sisters or mother or father or children or fields, for my sake and for the sake of the good news, who will not receive a hundredfold now in this age—houses, brothers and sisters, mothers and children, and fields, with persecutions— and in the age to come eternal life".[9]

Suffering

And suffering is what happens when we are persecuted for our faith. I sometimes wonder what would happen to the

---

[6] Gal 2:20 NASB
[7] Rom 6:11 NASB
[8] Lk 22:42
[9] Mark 10:29-30 NRSV

church in the West if we suffered true persecution, not just a little inconvenience or embarrassment for our faith, which is what most of us in the West experience from time to time, often thinking of it as persecution. For example, the rejection we may get when we share our faith, or the exclusion from the in-jokes at work because the others don't think we would appreciate them. It's hardly persecution.

But of course there are many parts of the world where people are being tortured or losing their lives for their faith on a regular basis. The Barnabas Aid magazine reports regularly on these persecuted Christians around the world.[10]

I wonder how the church in the UK would respond. Would it shrink drastically as in the USSR under communist oppression, or thrive as in the house church movement in China under the Maoist persecution?

Any army expects to serve the overall mission, to submit to authority, to surrender their rights to a comfortable life, to sacrifice for each other, and to suffer when needed. We naturally want to shy away from these 5S words. So let me leave you with these thoughts about them.

- The beauty of service = we discover our gifts and grow in the process
- The wisdom of submission = he knows best and we learn to trust
- The freedom of surrender = he takes responsibility and we breathe a sigh of relief
- The joy of sacrifice = he prepares a reward and we consider it a privilege
- The grace of suffering = he has suffered and we identify with him, making up what is lacking

---

[10] https://barnabasfund.org

And perseverance is always required.

Newt Gingrich, the American politician said 'Perseverance is the hard work you do after you get tired of doing the hard work you already did.'

And Thomas Edison, the inventor of the light bulb (among many other things) said 'Many of life's failures are people who did not realize how close they were to success when they gave up.'

Most human battles are not won overnight. They require exquisite preparation, training and orchestration, and getting food supply chains and ammunition supplies right. They are won as the troops dig in for what may be a prolonged conflict. They will involve losses and gains, but with good fortune the enemy will be gradually pushed back to the point of retreat or surrender.

So too with spiritual battles. We must be prepared, and we will need to persevere. The good news is that God's resources are infinitely greater than the enemy's, the enemy has already been defeated at the cross and we are simply the enforcers. Provided we stick to our confession of truth, our righteous lifestyle, remain under authority, and stay close to our precious sisters and brothers, we will have many great victories. And of course the ultimate destruction of Satan is assured – we know the end of the story![11]

Perseverance is required because we are in a battle. It is required because even though Satan was defeated at the cross, he is not yet destroyed, and thrashes around in his death throes trying to persuade us that he is still a viable entity; seeking to deceive us into agreeing with him and his

---

[11] Rev 20:10

deceitful lies, because only then can he exercise his malevolent influence over us.

God is not a combination of Google Home and Amazon Prime.

Perseverance is required because God's kingdom is not an instant society where everything happens at the push of a button. God is not a combination of Google Home and Amazon Prime. God is forming his character in us, and perseverance is growing it. See what the Apostle James had to say:

My fellow believers, when it seems as though you are facing nothing but difficulties see it as an invaluable opportunity to experience the greatest joy that you can! For you know that when your faith is tested it stirs up power within you to endure all things. And then as your endurance grows even stronger it will release perfection into every part of your being until there is nothing missing and nothing lacking.[12]

Questions:

- Have you ever experienced loss or difficulty because of your faith?
- How do you feel about the 5Ss?
- What areas of life are currently requiring perseverance?

---

[12] Jas 1:2-4 TPT

Part 4 – Disciple-making Disciples

So how does the Bride make herself ready? It's clearly something that is anticipated from the Apostle John's writing in Revelation.

Let us rejoice and be glad and give the glory to Him, for the marriage of the Lamb has come and His bride has made herself ready.[1]

It suggests that we are active participants in the bridal preparation process. We have something to do. Three of my four daughters are married and had wonderful weddings. None of them expected the process to be a passive one in which everything was done for them. As much as they needed help from others, they each took responsibility for making sure it all happened. So too, we are active participants in the 'Bride making herself ready'.

I'd suggest that there are two elements involved in this. When it comes to the Bride of Christ, her preparation is in two particular dimensions: his church is expected to grow in both quantity and quality. Both aspects are connected to the last words of Jesus in the Great Commission, in terms of disciple-making, and we will unpack that in this section.

His church is expected to grow in both quantity and quality.

---

[1] Rev 19:7 NASB

Chapter 13

Definition of A Disciple

Before we talk about quality or quantity, I guess if we are going to talk about making disciples, we ought to think about what we mean by the word *disciple*. There are a number of things I consider non-negotiable. The characteristics are listed below.

However, if I were to boil it down to one simple qualification it would be this: a disciple listens to what Jesus says, and does it. Jesus said that the wise man who builds his house

> *A disciple listens to what Jesus says, and does it.*

on a rock is the one who 'hears my words and puts them into practice'.[1] James, Jesus brother, put it this way, 'prove yourselves to be doers of the word, and not merely hearers who delude themselves'.[2] I fear there are many deluded people around who think of themselves as disciples, those who hold to a form of Christianity, but don't live as disciples.

Having said that, let's break down the characteristics into seven key attributes:

1. They are humble, teachable and have the heart of a learner. This is implicit in the Greek for the word

---

[1] Lk 6:46-49
[2] Jas 1:22 NASB

disciple, the word 'mathetes' which simply means a learner. How well do they listen, how attentive to God's voice are they? Do they seek out the wisdom of others?

2. They are becoming more like Jesus in his character and competencies. They are growing in the fruit of the Spirit – love, joy, peace, patience, kindness, goodness, faithfulness, gentleness and self-control. It's worth noting that most of these fruits are only grown in the context of relationships. It's very hard to grow in most of them without the pressure cooker of challenging relationships! Paul said to the Corinthians that they were to imitate him as he imitated Christ[3], and later that we would all be gradually transformed into his image.

And the Lord—who is the Spirit—makes us more and more like him as we are changed into his glorious image.[4]

They are also growing in confidence to do the things that Jesus did. Not only in the bold telling of good news, and compassion-motivated supernatural ministry, but also and perhaps most importantly of all, in making disciples and raising leaders. This was Jesus' main mission and activity over his three years of ministry. Jesus

> *The two abilities needed of all disciples are availability (lifestyle) and accountability (relationships).*

---

[3] 1 Cor 11:1 NLT
[4] 2 Cor 3:18b NLT

said that we would do the things he did.[5]

The two abilities needed of all disciples are availability (lifestyle) and accountability (relationships).

3. Availability – you discover how available you are when you find out how willing you are to be inconvenienced. The Father will nearly always inconvenience you in the early days of ministry. It's like he is saying 'are you sure you are up for this?' The Holy Spirit's adventures are nearly always unscheduled. Disciples are committed to being led by the Spirit[6], not dominated by the diary or agenda.

4. Accountability is measured by our willing vulnerability to let others speak into our lives, our openness in our progress in God's formational work in our lives, and our seeking out others to call us to account for what God is telling us to do. Do you have people who know everything there is to know about you and have the right to ask you the difficult questions at any time? We are not only called to live lives of accountability to our church leaders in general[7], but also to all those who help in the task of leading the church[8], those who as previously described act as spiritual parents to us.

5. They are growing in gospel and missional confidence and commitment. They are regularly telling their story to others who don't know him. They are good news people where they live, learn, work or play. They are

---

[5] Jn 14:12
[6] Rom 8:14
[7] Heb 13:17
[8] 1 Cor 16:16

ambassadors in their everyday lives for the kingdom of God.[9]

6. They have asked both 'to whom am I called?' and 'with whom am I called?' Recognising that being good news is not a solo sport, they are committed to finding out where they are being sent by God with the gospel, and with which tribe or people they are doing that. This may not all be immediately obvious, so the question needs to be asked regularly until clarity comes.[10]

7. They are committed to investing in others, both Christians and not-yet-Christians. They are looking to make disciples themselves. This will involve investing in the lives of those they believe God is drawing to himself, and in those who are seeking to grow as disciples.[11]

These characteristics are not exhaustive or complete, but a simple yardstick to see if what we are making is anything like the pattern of the New Testament disciple. This is not to condemn, but to highlight areas for growth.

One thing you could do with a potential disciple is to ask them to read through the above list, and ask them where they need help. This could then form the basis of an ongoing discipleship process, as well as showing how willing they are to be vulnerable and teachable in the first place.

---

[9] 2 Cor 5:20
[10] Jn 20:21
[11] Matt 28:19

Chapter 14

Growth in Quality

When we talk about discipleship, most people think about growing in maturity, and this is certainly a key part of the dynamic of discipleship.

We take as our source, both Jesus' example with, and his command to, his disciples.

The journey Jesus takes with his disciples is one of growing them into maturity. We see them at the start of their time with Jesus as raw recruits, just like army cadets on their first day in training – they need a lot of 'breaking in'. They are all over the place. They are impetuous, full of pride, power and position seeking, fearful and failing in their assignments, but when offered the chance to leave, the Apostle Peter responds with these well-known words,

"Lord, to whom shall we go? You have the words of eternal life."[1]

Peter didn't know much, but he did know that Jesus was the only one they wanted to be with. Each of us too has to make that same decision at some point. If we are to be disciples,

---

[1] Jn 6:68

we must commit ourselves to the journey of Jesus, and to the Jesus of the journey. He is the only one who can make something of us, who can bring us from our state of ignorance to a place of usefulness and maturity, who can see our

> *We must commit ourselves to the journey of Jesus, and to the Jesus of the journey.*

potential as human beings, created in God's image, fully developed. He knows us better than we know ourselves. His discipling of us is going to be so much more than any self-help development programme.

By the time we reach the day of Pentecost in Acts, we see a very different group of disciples. They are humbled by their failures, but wonderfully empowered by the Holy Spirit, bold and passionate, and dependent on the Lord Jesus.

At the end of his time with the disciples Jesus gives them this most famous command. We call it the great commandment. It appears in Luke's writing in Acts 1:8, in Mark's gospel in Mark 16:15, but we read it most clearly and explicitly in Matthew's gospel.

'Therefore go and make disciples of all nations, baptising them in the name of the Father and of the Son and of the Holy Spirit, and teaching them to obey everything I have commanded you. And surely I am with you always, to the very end of the age.'[2]

Colin Dye[3] describes this journey as one of Making, Marking, Maturing, Mobilising and Multiplying disciples.

- Making – bringing others to Jesus
- Marking – baptising them

---

[2] Matt 28:19-20
[3] Colin Dye is the Senior Leader of London City Church

- Maturing – teaching and training them
- Mobilising – getting them to obey, by doing what we have done
- Multiplying – the result of multiple generations of disciples doing the same thing

Maturing is a key part of the whole process of raising disciple-making disciples.

So how does this journey towards maturity as disciples happen? It doesn't take place by accident. Jesus works with his disciples over their three year internship in a very specific way. We describe this journey with a tool called the discipleship square, as covered in Reimagine Church.[4] In essence it's a process of the disciple watching, being taught, learning, having a go, being helped through times of failure, gaining the confidence to operate more independently, and finally being fully entrusted with the mission.

This process is not quick or easy. Most of us want to be instant experts, but because the goal is maturity, more than it is success, Jesus is willing to take time with us, ensuring that our character grows in line with our skills and experience. That's why we describe this journey as one of personal development in both character and competency.

The goal is maturity, more than it is success

The means and methods of this discipleship are not primarily Sunday sermons, training programmes, podcasts or personal study, although all of these can be helpful. It is more than anything a relationship or set of relationships through which spiritual formation takes place, just as it did with Jesus and his disciples. We sometimes liken it to an apprenticeship.

---

[4] See Reimagine Church, Nic Harding, Missio Publishing, p180-184

Apprentices learn mainly 'on the job', and so do disciples. Bringing a disciple to maturity is all about them learning through experience. It is about the necessity of failure, trying again until they succeed, and hammering out truth on the anvil of real life. Our mentors, coaches or guides on this journey are those God has placed in our lives for this season and for this purpose.

It's vital that we find those people God has called us to learn from, to be discipled by. As previously mentioned, the Greek word for disciple is the word 'mathetes' which literally means a learner or student. We are life-long learners or apprentices. We need others speaking into our lives for the whole of our lives. It saddens me when I meet those who clearly think they have nothing more to learn. They have ceased to be teachable. They have stopped asking questions. By my definition in the last section they have ceased to be disciples.

Some of our trainers are present for brief seasons; others become spiritual mothers and fathers to us for years or even decades. The ideal is that we find such spiritual parents within our everyday church family, the community of disciples we share life with. They have the chance to see us as we really are, not just the shiny version of us. They get to work with us in the local mission we are called to. They can help deploy us in stuff they are already involved in; that's how we get 'on the job training'. It's a win-win.

Our disciplers need access to our lives. They need our honesty and vulnerability. They need our cooperation in trying out new things. They need us to 'lean in' to all they have to offer us. They won't always be right and we need to be both teachable, but also willing to question, and to always take responsibility for our own decisions.

And so the journey continues, growing into the likeness of our ultimate discipler Jesus. We are being fashioned into his image. Uniquely ourselves, but universally like him![5]

As Dallas Willard says in The Divine Conspiracy 'Discipleship is the process of becoming who Jesus would be if he were you'.

As we grow to be more like Jesus, we also get to do more of the stuff that Jesus did. We grow in confidence and competence. It's part of the package. Jesus was clear that we would do what he did and even greater things.[6] How exciting is that!

For a period of time in my 20s, I was discipled by Steve Hepden, one of the leaders of the church that Jenny and I were part of in Bristol. I was still like wet cement, readily taking on the imprint of anyone who had something to teach me. This leader had a real ministry in deliverance, amongst other things. I hung around him whenever my medical jobs allowed. I was keen to learn. He let me get involved in praying for people. I was amazed to see them get free from long-standing demonic strongholds and attachments. It was an exciting time of growing in the competencies of Jesus.

It's really important that our ability to do Jesus' works is matched by our growth in his character. Too many, in pursuit of gifts, especially the more supernatural ones, have been shipwrecked by a lack of character, and the reputation of Jesus and his Bride has been damaged. We need both character and competency, and that's what growing in maturity, growth in quality involves.

---

[5] 2 Cor 3:18
[6] Jn 14:12

I am so grateful for those who have spoken into my life over many years, and for those who still do. One of my most painful 'ouch moment' memories is of a conversation with a wise man of God who was helping Jenny and I process our transition from Bristol to Liverpool. When sharing some of my frustrations with him, he replied, 'Nic, frustration is just another word for anger; what are you going to do about it?' Ouch! Others have pointed out my selfishness when I was justifying my actions as being in pursuit of what I thought was God's will. It turned out it was just my will; those who in my estimate were 'opposing the will of God', it transpired, were just blocking my personal goals. Ouch!

On another occasion I was in an ongoing dispute with one of my co-leaders. After getting nowhere, I asked advice from a friend who was a spiritual parent figure to me at that time. They said, 'Nic, you know you can win an argument and lose a friend.' I had been so determined to be proved right that I was even willing to do so at the expense of the relationship. Ouch!

It's not always easy to recognise these blind spots – that's why we need others who love us to help us and speak truth to us.

Becoming his Bride, the church that Jesus died for and is coming back for will involve some painful growing up. It will at times challenge our independence, and certainly our individualism and consumerism. Our self-will will be conformed to his will. Our selfishness will give way to others-centredness. Our self-sufficiency will morph into a Jesus dependency. Our hard-heartedness will give way to his compassion. Our love of comfort will make way for the joy of service. Pleasure-seeking will decrease and joy-bringing will increase. Life will be full in every sense of the word!

There are plenty of more tools for growing disciples in *Reimagine Church.*[7]

Questions:

- What or who has been the most formative influence on your growth into maturity as a disciple?
- Who is currently 'speaking into your life'?
- What areas of your character or competencies do you want to grow in? Be as specific as possible.

———————————————

[7] Reimagine Church, Nic Harding, Missio Publishing (especially Section 2)

Chapter 15

Growth In Quantity

Just as disciple-making involves growth in quality, it also involves growth in quantity. We saw that the great commission can be unpacked into the 5Ms of making, marking, maturing, mobilising and multiplying disciples. The latter two of these, mobilising and multiplying, are all about increase in quantity.

You see Jesus doesn't just want to come back for a Bride who is mature, but small in number, he wants a Bride that numbers in the billions. In fact we know from the book of Revelation that this Bride will be representative of every people group on the face of the earth. Jesus wants multitudes.

After this I looked, and there before me was a great multitude that no one could count, from every nation, tribe, people and language, standing before the throne and before the Lamb. They were wearing white robes and were holding palm branches in their hands.[1]

What a great description of the Bride of Christ, the white robes of maturity and purity, but also multitudes. Multitudes from every people group on earth, diversity worshipping in unity around the throne of God, before the lover of their souls, the awesome Bridegroom, the Lamb of God.

---

[1] Rev 7:9

It's worth adding in here that the pastors, teachers and prophets to which Eph 4 refers, tend to be more focussed on quality. Evangelists and apostles tend to be more focussed on quantity, on extension, and on multiplication of disciples, communities and churches. That's why we need each other.

The apostle Paul is clear when writing to Timothy that God 'wants all people to be saved and come to a knowledge of the truth'.[2] And the Apostle Peter is equally clear when writing to Jewish and Gentile Christians in Asia Minor, that God is 'not wishing for any to perish but for all to come to repentance.'[3]

I don't know what your definition of 'all' is, but in my dictionary it means all! Whatever your views on the sovereignty of God, the election of the saints, or on predestination may be; one thing I know is that God does not wilfully exclude anyone from a relationship with himself, or from a place in eternity with him and his Bride. His heart is completely the opposite. If it were possible, he would take everyone with him.

Our job then, if you like, is to maximise the opportunity for exactly that to happen. We are commanded to go and make disciples in every nation, the Greek word for nation, 'ethnos', literally 'a distinct people group'. If God's heart is for every woman, man and child, then so is ours. We have no freedom to only look for people like us, for the nice, polite, well behaved people, but also for those who do not come in well-presented packages, those who are different to us, those who we don't easily understand or relate to, but those whom God has also created in his image and dearly loves.

If we are in the business of Bridal maximisation, then what does that look like?

---

[2] 1 Tim 2:4
[3] 2 Pet 3:9 NASB

It starts with each one of us who have heard the invitation from Jesus to 'follow me', to also hear the rest of the challenge which is 'and I will make you fishers of men'.[4] For those who have responded to the 'come here', to also respond to the 'go there'. We are both a called people and a sent people. As Jesus puts it,

'As the Father has sent me, I am sending you.'[5]

We are sent to a broken and hurting world. We are called to reach out to the least, the last and the lost. We are called to be, do, and say good news to our neighbour, whoever or wherever they may be. We prayerfully, lovingly, patiently and courageously become witnesses and ambassadors wherever we go, wherever we live, learn, work or play.[6]

> We are called to be, do, and say good news

Being good news is about our lifestyle of love and integrity, it's about others being able to see something different about us in the way we live. People notice it when we are different.

Doing good news is about the demonstration of the good news of the kingdom through our simple daily acts of kindness, or through those more organised ministries that are reaching out to people with practical needs, through things like foodbanks, street pastors and debt advice.

Doing good news is also about our faith for the supernatural in the lives of those we are reaching out to. This might for example be in praying for healing with someone who is sick, bringing a word of knowledge that encourages the person we

---

[4] Matt 4:19 NASB
[5] Jn 20:21
[6] Acts 1:8, 2 Cor 5:20

are with to know that God is interested in them, or just praying for the person to experience God's peace in a difficult time.

Being competent and confident to move in the supernatural dimension is a key part to growing as a disciple. We need to find those who can mentor us in this dimension so that it becomes a normal part of everyday life. There is no doubt in my mind that without the supernatural kingdom manifestations of healing and deliverance from evil spirits, Jesus' ministry would never have taken off. He would never have raised twelve world-changing disciples. The supernatural was key to all Jesus accomplished. And as Jesus said, 'it is enough for the disciple that he become as his teacher'.[7]

Saying good news is obviously about speaking about Jesus and our faith. It's about sharing our story with others and seeing if they want to know more. It's about being able to tell God's better story that they are invited into.

There is a journey involved in the making of disciples who become disciple-makers. I call it (surprisingly) the Disciple-Makers Journey. Details can be found in *Reimagine Church*.[8]

The family network of leaders and churches that I have the privilege of giving direction to is called Kairos Connexion (Kx).[9] Our strapline is 'raising missionary disciples'. This is another way of saying 'raising disciples who make disciple-makers'. Before we can raise disciples to maturity, mobilise them and see them multiply, we have to 'make' them, to bring them to Christ in the first place. We have to reach out to lost

---

[7] Matt 10:25 NASB

[8] Reimagine Church, Nic Harding, Missio Publishing. Chapter 6

[9] www.kairosconnexion.org

people. We have to be, do and say good news to them, wherever they live, learn, work and play.

We need both gospel and missional confidence. Kx provides training for this. We have discovered that most people, even seasoned church leaders lack both. We train people to be able to share their story in 2-3 minutes, to have easy ways to talk about Jesus, to introduce others to their church family, to find the people of peace that the Spirit is already working in[10] (those who are leaning into relationship with us and are spiritually open), and to take them on a spiritual journey of discovery.

As they come to faith, they are also introduced to the disciple-makers journey. They bring others with them on that same journey. They become disciples who make disciples. They are mobilised to become first witnesses, then disciple-makers, and then multipliers.

They are mobilised to become first witnesses, then disciple-makers, and then multipliers..

I had the joy of leading a young man to Christ early on in my medical career. I was getting a name plate made for my medical practice. This man owned the industrial engraving business that I went to. He was also called Nick. From that began a friendship that has lasted nearly 40 years. Nick was quick to see that God was at work in his work force and a number of them in time gave their lives to Christ too. Some of those workers have also gone on to lead others to Christ. That's multiplication. Disciples who make disciples.

This journey of course is never a solo event. If we were to use a sports metaphor, it's not an athletics match where each

---

[10] Luke 10:1-11

athlete competes for himself or herself, for individual gold. It is more like a soccer match, where each player works together towards a common goal – that of scoring a goal! The team competes not for individual medals, but for a shared cup.

The metaphor of a shared cup has implications for us as his Bride. It's a cup not only of celebration in victory, but also a cup of suffering, the cost of that victory. Or perhaps the cup of the new covenant that we will share with him in his Father's kingdom, when the Bridegroom will once again taste the fruit of the vine with his Bride on his great and glorious wedding day.[11] That's a cup worth sacrificing for!

So for each of us, as we find our place in that radical community, that invincible army, we work together for shared victory and common goals. We see our task of being a good news people as something we do together. We pray together; we share connection with each other's people of peace; we play our different parts in the body, enabling new believers to grow in their faith. Together we provide a warm, inclusive, hope-filled environment in which to invite the spiritual seeker. It's a together thing; it's a family thing.

This takes the stress out of winning others to Christ. We do it together. It takes the pressure out of caring for new believers who probably have some big needs. We do it together. It takes the strain out of having to be all things to everyone. We are the body of Christ who work as one.

For all the people who have come to Christ in recent years through our missional community it's never been a pressure on any one person. Some are better at making the initial contact. Some find inviting easy. Others share Jesus more naturally. Some are better at providing hospitality. Some are

---

[11] Matt 26:29

great at getting alongside the new person, one on one. Others are better at consistent input, opening the scriptures and training new believers.

I remember well a Muslim Somali asylum seeker who was invited to and came to faith in our missional community one night. He was with us for a year (before the government moved him to the North East). He pretty much had every need known to man. But between us we helped with his needs around language, transport, housing, food, access to legal support, medical issues, and of course growing in his faith. To name but a few! The community pulled together and no one was burned out in the process.

He sat around our table for weeks saying very little, till one night when we were in the middle of a discovery Bible study, he stopped us and said, 'You know, I see you are very happy,' (he obviously wasn't). 'I think it's because you have Jesus, can I have him?' Well that was a profound moment for all of us, as you can imagine.

He was led to Christ and baptised. He grew in his faith. His needs were gradually met, and by the time he was moved away by the government hc was ready to be connected with a new church.

The Bridegroom is not satisfied with a few, but longs for multitudes to make up his glorious Bride. We are entrusted with growing that Bride, not only in quality but also in quantity.

The Bridegroom is not satisfied with a few, but longs for multitudes to make up his glorious Bride.

We get to see the multiplication of disciples, communities and ultimately churches.

Questions:

- What part have you had in seeing others come to faith in Christ? And how did it feel when they gave their lives to Christ?
- How confident do you feel in the gospel, or of living missionally?
- How could you be further equipped to become a disciple-maker?

Chapter 16

Disciple-Making Movements

There has been a lot written on both disciple-making and church planting movements. Most of the data and stories have come from developing nations, primarily from parts of Asia and sub-Saharan Africa. The rate of spread of the gospel has been staggering. It mirrors some of the explosive growth of the Chinese House Church movement, and the early church. Much of this has been documented in David Garrison's *Church Planting Movements*[1], Jerry Trousdale's *Miraculous Movements*[2], and in T4T *A Discipleship Re-revolution* by Steve Smith with Ying Kai.[3]

There have been many attempts to contextualise these approaches for Western Culture, and while there are some stories of encouragement, there seems to be very little evidence that the same methodology is producing the same levels of breakthrough in our Western culture. I have been forced to admit that methodology is not the answer.

---

[1] Church Planting Movements, David Garrison, How God is Redeeming a Lost World, WIGTake resources 2004
[2] Miraculous Movements, Jerry Trousdale, Thomas Nelson. 2012
[3] T4T A Discipleship Re-revolution, Steve Smith with Ying Kai, WIGTake Resources. 2011

We have much to learn from these disciple-making movements.

Whilst I do believe we have much to learn from these disciple-making movements (DMMs), We cannot yet expect the same results in the West. We absolutely do need the same levels of passionate commitment to the cause of Christ and boldness with the gospel. We will need the same kind of strategic approach that will help build pipelines of leaders and multiply small groups. We of course need the same levels of commitment to prayer and fasting, spiritual warfare and supernatural expectancy. And then... maybe, just maybe...

But my instinct is that even then we will not see the same kinds of breakthrough. I believe that until the church and the world we live in are brought to their knees through persecution, national instability, war, disease, or economic collapse, we will not see the same impact (this was written before anyone in the UK had heard about Coronavirus). There is something about the soil in which we are sowing gospel seed that is just not as receptive as these other parts of the world. We are just too comfortable, both world and church.

We often quote the scripture where Jesus says that 'the harvest is plentiful... Ask the Lord of the harvest, therefore, to send out more workers into his harvest field'[4], or where he says that 'the fields are ripe for harvest'.[5] We use this to try and convince ourselves that this is truo in our local Western Culture context. I'm not convinced it is just yet. When Jesus said those words he was speaking to a specific context where his ministry of miracles had been drawing huge crowds. There were more people seeking Jesus than could be handled. The harvest really was plentiful – there and then.

---

[4] Lk 10:2
[5] Jn 4:35

And it clearly is plentiful in many parts of the world today. And I pray and believe it will soon be in our Western context too. But I don't see it yet.

So I've stopped beating myself up about the small harvests that we are seeing. I'm listening to Zechariah and his words to the Israelites when there wasn't much to show for all their hard work, '[Don't] despise the day of small things'.[6] And, yes, I'm believing and working for so much more.

> '[Don't] despise the day of small things'

So what can we learn from the DMMs that can help us maximise the opportunities that do exist, and the potential for making disciples-makers? Here are some key principles that we find embedded in the way that DMMs operate.

1. The gospel is for everyone, not just a few.
   This is key for those in the rapidly multiplying movements of disciple-making. The implications are that, having 'our feet fitted with the readiness that comes from the gospel of peace'[7], we are to be ready to 'make the most of every opportunity'.[8] The question that immediately comes to mind is 'what constitutes an opportunity?'

   I have encountered utterly driven evangelists who only have one kind of conversation with anyone they meet. It is a gospel conversation, and it is often done in a quite abrasive, insensitive and at times even offensive way. It fails to give the person the dignity of being a human being who is worthy of love, of being known and understood, and of being invited into a

---

[6] Zech 4:10
[7] Eph 6:15
[8] Col 4:5

relationship. I think it often does the cause of the gospel harm, because of the way the encounter alienates the person involved.

By way of contrast however the opposite problem is more the norm in our culture – an unwillingness to say anything to anyone of a spiritual nature, for fear of offending, of embarrassment, or of rejection. This is equally a strategy of the enemy for emasculating the gospel, and getting us to hide our lights under bowls.[9]

We have to find the balance, in both being ready at all times, not being held back by fear of embarrassment or rejection, and also of treating people with dignity and respect, offering the chance for a relational connection before introducing spiritual truth to the conversation. The person of peace principle[10] seems to get this about right. Everyone heard, but not everyone was invested in when Jesus sent his disciples out to preach the gospel in the towns and villages. We need to be ready to make a friendly connection with everyone we meet. We need a willingness to take the conversation further and even to a spiritual topic if possible. We also need to build on the relationship if there is openness to us and to spiritual things. I call this the 3Be's of finding people of peace:

...Be friendly – say hi

...Be curious – find out about them, show genuine interest

...Be ready – with your story or gospel truth

---

[9] Matt 5:15

[10] Lk 10:1-11. See Reimagine Church (Ch 6), Nic Harding, Missio publishing

2. Letting God speak for himself.

   He is at work in many individuals and we need to find them. Again the person of peace principle undergirds this. But we can also invite someone to a way of exploring scripture where God can speak to the person directly. This is a way of letting God speak, draw, convict and save. We sometimes refer to this as Discovery Bible Study (DBS) and obedience based discipleship. The keys are firstly that we believe that the seeker can and will hear God for themselves through the Bible passage. And secondly that once they have heard God, they can be offered a place of accountability for seeing through what God has asked them to do. This potentially builds a pattern of obedience-based discipleship rather than convenience-based

   > *This potentially builds a pattern of obedience-based discipleship rather than convenience-based discipleship.*

   discipleship. The latter simply says 'I'll obey if it suits me'. DMMs make good use of Discovery Bible Study principles.

3. Natural networks Many of us have some difficulty in finding new people to connect with around the gospel; mainly because we don't have many non-Christian friends left by the time we have been Christians for 5 years or more. The new believer by contrast often has a huge natural network of not-yet-Christian connections. The key here is to find ways of connecting with the new believer's network very early on. Firstly in getting the new believer to share their own story with that network, and secondly in offering people from that network to host something like a Discovery Bible Study for themselves. So when

someone comes to Christ, we very simply ask if we can meet their friends. From there it's only a short step to offer a DBS and from that find out if there are any people of peace in that group. If so they can be invited to follow Christ too. This is typically how DMMs operate. We sometimes describe this as going on their terms and their turf. It's a key to multiplication. The new believer is a door to a whole new extended family or community.

Typically, churches expect a not-yet-Christian to come to our events where they won't know anyone, won't understand what is going on, and will feel like they stand out like a sore thumb, and then we expect them to enjoy every moment of it. This is 'our terms' (we make the rules) and 'our turf' (we rule the territory). It's much more fruitful, respectful and useful to go to their territory, and play by their rules if possible.

4. Organic systems
   This is the term that Alan Hirsch uses in 'The Forgotten Ways'[11] when he is describing one of the 6 main strands of the apostolic DNA of church planting movements, or what he calls mDNA, missional or movemental DNA.

   Organic systems is a phrase that describes how we put all the pieces of the jigsaw together. The strategic and tactical, the equipping and training elements, the tools, vehicles and process parts. Organic suggests that it has a life of its own; that it is a living thing that will keep moving or growing without massive administrative or organisational initiative being taken,

---

[11] The Forgotten Ways. Alan Hirsch, Brazos Press. See chapter 7

without centralised control. That it has a natural life cycle where reproduction takes place, and leads over time to multiplication. It leads to simple reproducible systems and structures, led from the bottom up, not the top down.

5. Rapid multiplication of small or mid-sized groups
   This is essential to both retain and disciple new converts, and to provide a context in which new leaders of other small groups can be identified and trained.

I believe that we must take these convictions and principles from DMM practice, and inculcate them into the way we do church in the West.

If we want the bride of Christ to be both massive (multitudes), and all pervasive (every people group), then we need to embrace these ideas from the DMMs that God is blessing unbelievably in other parts of the world.

Questions:

- Why do you think that the rapid multiplication of disciples and groups being seen in other parts of the world isn't happening here yet?
- How do you feel about the statement that the gospel is for all, not just a few?

Part 5 – End-Times Orientation

Eschatology is the study of the end-times. They culminate with Jesus' return and the final judgement. The new heavens and the new earth are revealed, and Jesus the Bridegroom comes to claim his beautiful Bride.

I hope that all through this book I have been successfully making the case that the development of the church now needs to be seen in the light of the future Bride of Christ. This is our ultimate goal, and it needs to shape all that we do here and now.

As I said in the introduction, so much of church leadership, church involvement and church development is expedient. It is responding to immediate pressure, to the latest fashions of the day, and to what we as leaders think is expected of us. What would it look like for that great and final day to shape all that we did in the here and now? For church to be prepared as a Bride, in holy and breath-holding expectation of that day?

> *What would it look like for that great and final day to shape all that we did in the here and now?*

Chapter 17

The Already and The Not Yet

I've already referred to the book of New Testament Theology by George Eldon Ladd[1] and his ideas about the breaking in of God's kingdom in the here and now, and the final consummation of that kingdom on the day of his return. It's important to recognise the two main errors in regard to this – if you like, the two ditches on either side of the eschatological highway of the kingdom.

On the one side is the ditch of 'the not yet'. This ditch is characterised by a church who envisages all the breaking in of the kingdom and the consummation of that kingdom as a future event. It assigns what happens on the earth now as being of little importance. This leads to a 'bunker mentality' where we just get our ticket to heaven and wait it out until everything is destroyed and the new heavens and earth appear, in which we will be forever with Christ in his eternal kingdom. This was a more historic view in much of the twentieth century. It is less prevalent today.

This ditch leads to a lack of care for the earth, little motivation for evangelism or concern for reforming the cultures and structures of our society along kingdom lines. It also leads to a reduction of the gospel to a ticket to heaven. In other words, "Say this prayer and you will be saved". It is a travesty of all

---

[1] George Eldon Ladd, A Theology of the New Testament, James Clarke and Co Ltd

that Jesus demonstrated and taught about his kingdom. He showed that the kingdom may not be universally accepted, but it was to be the salt of our society and the light of our world. It was anticipated that as more and more people turned to Christ that the places in which we lived would also be transformed. And this is what church history has borne out in so many places and times.

The work of the Bride 'making herself ready' is not just personal sanctification, but also disciple-making proliferation, and town and city transformation.

Jesus taught his disciples to pray, "Your kingdom come and your will be done on earth as it is in heaven". We are to expect that the kingdom breaking in is having a here-and-now effect, for the betterment of our places – our communities, workplaces, villages, towns and cities. We are to not only pray, but also to work to that end as led and empowered by the Spirit of God. The work of the Bride 'making herself ready' is not just personal sanctification, but also disciple-making proliferation, and town and city transformation.

The other ditch is the 'already' ditch. In this ditch we see that the kingdom is already here in its fullness, even if perhaps not yet fully manifest. But the feeling is that it's just a question of time. If we wait long enough, the kingdom will gradually take over our places. Kingdom rule will be expressed in cities and nations and they will come fully under the rule of Christ in this age. Christ will return to that fully realised kingdom. If you like, he becomes just the icing on the cake.

This ditch leads to a set of false expectations. It would expect the rule of God's kingdom to gradually take over earthly governments, businesses and social structures. It would work towards that end. It might expect Christians to be in charge, maybe to reinstate some Old Testament laws in which sinful people would be punished for the errancy of their ways. It would be a heavenly kingdom with earthly legal reinforcement. This view gained some popularity in the late twentieth century under authors like Rousas Rushdoony and what was called Christian Reconstructionism.

This would also likely lead to a lot of judgementalism and self-righteousness. It would not be a pretty sight. This would be a fully realised 'kingdom now' perspective, and I don't think that scripture gives any indication that this will happen. In fact, the end times seem more than anything to be full of warnings about a great falling away, an apostasy, great persecution and deception of God's people.[2] Hardly the kingdom in all its fullness.

This 'kingdom now' perspective could also connect with false ideas of the new heavens and new earth. It could lead to an unhelpful pressure to preserve the fabric of the earth at all costs. Don't get me wrong, we are called to steward our planet well. We only have one earth. So all efforts to deal with pollution, climate change, and preservation of natural resources are to be commended and supported.

But when Jesus returns there will be a destroying or freeing of the earth, depending on how you translate the word in 2 Peter 3. Let's take a look at this key verse:

But the day of the Lord will come like a thief. The heavens will disappear with a roar; the elements will be destroyed by fire, and the earth and everything done in it will be laid bare.[3]

The word destroyed, Greek 'luo' is more normally translated 'loose from bondages, or untie'; suggesting that the purpose of the fire is to reveal what has been hidden and previously

---

[2] Matt 24
[3] 2 Pet 3:10

corrupted by sin. The Apostle Paul also speaks of this in his letter to the Romans:

..that the creation itself will be liberated from its bondage to decay and brought into the freedom and glory of the children of God.[4]

> Whatever damage has been done by sin, original, historic and current, will be undone.

It seems that the fire of judgement will not in fact totally destroy or do away with the heavens and the earth, but will set them free from the corruption of sin back into their original purpose; hence the new, or perhaps renewed, heavens and earth of 2 Pet 3. God's children will get their new resurrection bodies on that day[5], so it seems does the earth. Whatever damage has been done by sin, original, historic and current, will be undone.

The preceding passage[6] talks about the purging of the earth by the flood when God also judged the sinfulness of mankind. The earth remained but it was purged. I imagine Christ's second coming in judgement will do the same. Then it was by water; in the future it will be by fire.

So there is a cataclysmic event of judgement that will be with literal or metaphorical fire. In this judgement, not only will mankind be judged but so too will Satan and the demonic realm.[7] But there will also be a significant change in the nature or substance of the earth.

---

[4] Rom 8:21 NIV
[5] 1 Cor 15:42-53
[6] 2 Pet 3:5-6
[7] Rev 20:1-15

Peter talks about 'the new heavens and the new earth', new in kind or substance.[8] In the same way, Jesus still had a body after his death and resurrection, but it was different in substance. He was recognisable by the piercings of his hands and side.[9] He was able to eat and drink with them.[10] But he was also able to materialise in rooms without going through the doors[11], he was able to appear and disappear in places instantly.[12]

So if the earth is to be set free, liberated, revealed for what it was always intended to be, it seems clear that the effects of sin on the earth, whether that be on the natural order i.e. earthquakes, floods and natural disasters, from the effect of man's pollution and pillage of its natural resources, or whatever kind of corruption and degradation, that this will be undone on the day of judgement. Hallelujah!

I say all this to make clear the point that while the environmental message is important, the new heavens and new earth are not dependent on our right use of plastics or eco-friendly products. We do this because it is good stewardship of the natural resources entrusted to us by God. We do good creation care because it was part of Adam and Eve's original mandate. It respects the gift given to us by the Lord, not because by doing so we are in some way preparing the new heavens and earth.

We also exercise good governance of our planet because it is 'training for reigning' in the eternal kingdom.[13]

---

[8] 2 Pet 3:13
[9] Jn 20:20
[10] Acts 10:40-41
[11] Jn 20:19, 26
[12] Lk 24:31
[13] Rev 5:10

It is the 'kingdom now but also the kingdom still to come'.

So what is the place of healthy tension and balance? Surely it is the 'kingdom now but also the kingdom still to come'. It is the already and the not yet, the increasing breaking in of God's kingdom through our prayers and actions, but not in completion. We recognise in this age, before Christ returns, that it will not be in fullness, but in a measure.

Someone asked Bill Johnson[14] how much of God's kingdom will we see in this present age. I liked his reply. He said, 'Well, how much do you want to see?'

When the Apostle Paul talks to the church in Corinth about spiritual gifts he says that what we have now is only partial, it is imperfect. That which is perfect is yet to come.

Now our knowledge is partial and incomplete, and even the gift of prophecy reveals only part of the whole picture! But when the time of perfection comes, these partial things will become useless.[15]

Similarly, with all the manifestations of God's kingdom breaking in, what we have now is partial and incomplete. The perfect and complete come when the Bride and Bridegroom are united at Jesus' return. That's why it's worth waiting for and worth working for.

Questions:

- Which of the two ditches are you more likely to fall into and why?

---

[14] Senior Pastor of Bethel Church, Redding California
[15] 1 Cor 13:9-10 NLT

- How are your prayers, choices, relationships, work, commitments, lifestyle and priorities bringing in the kingdom?

Chapter 18

THE BRIDE MAKES HERSELF READY

Having made the distinction between disciples growing in quality and quantity in Part 4, it's important to recognise that these two things are perfectly integrated and mutually interdependent.

Firstly, because disciples who have no strength of maturity, no deep love for Christ, no development of character, are unlikely to be able to sustain the motivation required for the disciple-maker's journey, the bringing in and discipling of multitudes. It is a process that will involve a heart of service and willingness to sacrifice, and that is unlikely to be forthcoming in an immature, self-oriented disciple, especially if they are still in a consumer mindset. As they mature, they take on more and more of those things that concern Christ. They become more committed to pleasing him in all they do. In other words, the quest for quality, will underpin the journey towards quantity.

> *The quest for quality, will underpin the journey towards quantity.*

Secondly, it is in the act of embracing the great commission of going and making disciples, that the new believer will find the necessity of drawing on Christ's strength and power. In other words, the embracing of the mission will automatically lead to a growing in maturity. Their prayer life will grow. Their cooperation with others who are sharing in that mission will grow. Their understanding of their unique gifts and contribution to the mission will grow. Most people who have been on a short-term mission report that they grow in their relationship with Christ in that context much faster than at most other times. In other words, seeking quantity provokes the formation of quality.

Maturity, and mission that leads to multiplication are inextricably interlinked, as we saw in the 5Ms of the great commission. So there is no false dichotomy in this eschatological perspective. The Bride will grow in both quality and quantity in the light of Jesus' soon return.

In fact if we take the famous words of Jesus from Matt 24 about the signs of the end, when he will return, words I sometimes call 'the great completion', we see that he won't return until the job is complete, and the Bride has finished the job of reaching every person and people group with the gospel. Jesus said,

'And the Good News about the Kingdom will be preached throughout the whole world, so that all nations will hear it; and then the end will come.'[1]

This quantitative process of completing the great commission is the qualitative equivalent of the 'Bride making herself ready'.[2] There is no competition; they are one and the same process.

So we come to the great wedding day. The day in which Bride and Groom will be fully united, their relationship will be celebrated, and with marriage being the prime metaphor for this relationship, it's impossible to imagine that it won't be with a great wedding feast. We know that Jesus talked about drinking the fruit of the vine when he comes again in his father's kingdom.[3] We know that Jesus cooked a meal and

[1] Matt 24:14 NLT
[2] Rev 19:7
[3] Matt 26:29

shared it with his disciples after his resurrection on the beach by Galilee. Of his return Jesus said,

I say to you that many will come from the east and the west, and will take their places at the feast with Abraham, Isaac and Jacob in the kingdom of heaven.[4]

And there are a number of parables told by Jesus that have eschatological connections – the parable of the wedding feast[5], the parable of the faithful servant[6], and the parable of the ten virgins.[7]

Jesus' return was of uttermost importance to him. He wanted the church, his Bride to be ready. He wanted us to be awake and appropriately clothed. In the book of Revelation, marriage and weddings are unsurprisingly the dominant theme for understanding the relationship between the Bride and Groom.

Let us rejoice and be glad and give him glory! For the wedding of the Lamb has come, and his bride has made herself ready.[8]

So how do we prepare for the wedding? The Apostle Peter summed it up well when he asked the question, in the light of Jesus' soon return, 'what sort of people ought we to be?'. His reply to his own question was,

---

[4] Matt 8:11
[5] Matt 22:1-14
[6] Matt 24:42-51
[7] Matt 25:1-13
[8] Rev 19:7

...don't you see how vital it is to live a holy life? We must be consumed with godliness while we anticipate and help to speed up the coming of the day of God...[9]

So we are not only to look to hasten or speed up the day of his coming by completing the work he has given us to do (the great commission to the great completion), but also to set ourselves apart for him in holiness and godliness. Holiness and godliness don't generally get people really excited do they? They are often looked on with some suspicion as the preserve of the 'super-spiritual' or the self-righteous. But nothing could be further from the truth.

Holiness is not only something imputed to us through the cross of Christ[10], it is also something that grows in us through our choices and commitments. It is the holiness without which none of us will see the Lord. [11] This holiness is sometimes called sanctification, the process of becoming more like Christ in our everyday lives, attitudes, words, thoughts and actions. It is the holiness that sets us free from the addictive power of sin, from the false identities that we construct for ourselves, from the insecurity and inferiority that we often grow up with. Why? Because holiness is wholeness. Godliness is goodness. We want both.

Sin devours our relationships, damages our health and mental well-being, and robs us of our destiny. Satan (the thief) comes to steal, kill and destroy, but Jesus says he has come to give us life in its fullness, abundance and richness.[12] Everything else is just counterfeit, promising much but delivering little of lasting value. Sin may be something done to us, or something we choose. The results are somewhat

---

[9] 2 Pet 3:11-12 TPT
[10] 2 Cor 5:21
[11] Heb 12:14
[12] Jn 10:10

similar. Jesus has come to offer us his healing and freedom, his meaning and purpose, his love and acceptance, his identity and destiny. Sanctification is a liberation destination.

The Bride of Christ is meant to be good news – in fact, is called to be, do and say good news. The good news is an invitation to freedom you could never attain, forgiveness you could never deserve and fulfillment you could never imagine.

Freedom you could never attain
It's freedom from self-obsession and narcissism (it's all about me); from the insecurity and brokenness of not having been loved or valued by parents; from the addiction to pleasure or comfort seeking to fill the inner void that the lack of unconditional affirming love has left; freedom to be who God meant you to be; freedom from shame, worthlessness and inadequacy, from the fear that I don't have what it takes or am not loveable. That's real freedom!

Forgiveness you could never deserve
It's a clean conscience from the nagging doubt that you have not met the grade, or have offended the one who made you, and therefore deserve some kind of punishment. We are released from the guilt we have tried unsuccessfully to bury through denial, self-justification, or blame of others. It's forgiveness from those things we have said, thought or done for which we can never make amends. No one else but Jesus can give that forgiveness.

Fulfillment you could never imagine
It comes in discovering your unique shape and purpose in God's design; in the significance of God's call on your life; in the distinct personality and set of gifts he has given you. It's fulfillment from the long-term relationships in which he has set you; in the opportunities he has given you to serve and give to others. It's fulfillment in knowing the Father in heaven, from simply being unconditionally loved as his child and now

being part of his incredible family, his church. And it's in being prepared for a wedding day as a spotless and beautiful Bride.

That's why we call it good news, and the more we pursue holiness and godliness, the more of this good news, this freedom, forgiveness and fulfillment we get to experience.

Brides spend much time in the build-up to the wedding in planning and preparation, but in the immediate run-up to the day there is a whole lot of pampering going on. Facials, massages, toning, perhaps weight loss (to get into the wedding dress chosen 12 months previously), manicures, pedicures, and of course the hair and make-up on the day.

All this is to look at her best for her bridegroom, and for her family and friends. We want to be at our best spiritually for our Bridegroom Jesus, the Lamb of God, and for our spiritual family on the wedding day.

Holiness and godliness are our friends. Pursuing holiness and godliness is not for the faint-hearted or the half-hearted. It is for the courageous, for the determined, for the humble, and those who have come to know their need of Jesus. Holiness and godliness are our friends. Why not make friends with them today? Start by welcoming them into your life. Ask Jesus to increase your appetite for them, and reduce your dependence on those things that compromise, pollute and damage you. Ask him to show you his way, his better way as you make decisions and take action in the coming days.

We know that when he returns we will all be changed in the twinkling of an eye.[13] And we know that that will, at the very least, be from earthly bodies to heavenly resurrection bodies.

---

[13] I Cor 15:52

Does it also include character transplants? Does it mean that we will all become super-lovely godly people? It's hard to imagine that it doesn't mean that. But could our level of earthly sanctification not only be linked to our heavenly reward[14], and responsibility[15], but also to our spiritual state and status in heaven? We will find out sooner or later. I for one want to be ready!

Questions:

- How prepared would you feel if you knew Jesus was coming back tomorrow?
- What things would you want to work on and change?
- How could you cooperate with others for the completion of the great commission?

---

[14] 2 Cor 5:10
[15] Lk 19:17, 19

Chapter 19

The Hope of Heaven

For most people who were part of the New Testament church their lives were shaped directly by two future things. First the imminent return of Christ, and secondly the expectation of being with him in heaven. The Apostle Paul put it this way when writing to the church at Colossae:

For we have heard of your faith in Christ Jesus and your love for all of God's people, which come from your confident hope of what God has reserved for you in heaven. You have had this expectation ever since you first heard the truth of the Good News.[1]

Their behaviour (the love for all God's people) was directly related to their great hope of heaven. Today this has largely been lost to the church. We tend to live for the day, or for shorter-term earthly goals as in family and career, or for plans to grow and develop our churches (if you are a church leader). Why is this so?

> *Their behaviour was directly related to their great hope of heaven.*

I believe that we have lost this eschatological focus and motivation because firstly we rarely preach about it, secondly we don't pray about Jesus' return, and thirdly we don't consciously and cooperatively work for the completion of the

---

[1] Col 1:4-5 NLT

great commission, the one event that will trigger the series of events culminating in Christ's return. We have to regain this passion and focus if we are to truly become the Bride of Christ, the church that Jesus died for and is coming back for. She will only fully embrace the 5Ss of service, submission, surrender, sacrifice and suffering if she has this heavenly perspective.

When we compare the minor inconveniences or even the significant sacrifices we make with the glory of heaven to come, and with the incredible joy of being with Jesus face to face, it will seem like nothing. We'll think, 'Why did I make such a fuss? Why did I resist those choices that could have so furthered the kingdom and helped to prepare the Bride?' It will all seem very insignificant looking back from the perspective of heaven.

When we look at the early church we see a group of people whose view of heaven was so real, that they were even able to give up their lives gladly. Stephen the first Christian martyr was one such person. We read about his encounter with the religious leaders in Acts 7.

When they heard these things, they were overtaken with violent rage filling their souls, and they gnashed their teeth at him. But Stephen, overtaken with great faith, was full of the Holy Spirit. He fixed his gaze into the heavenly realm and saw the glory and splendour of God—and Jesus, who stood up at the right hand of God.
"Look!" Stephen said. "I can see the heavens opening and the Son of Man standing at the right hand of God to welcome me home!"
His accusers covered their ears with their hands and screamed at the top of their lungs to drown out his voice. Then they pounced on him and threw him outside the city walls to stone him. His accusers, one by one, placed their outer garments at the feet of a young man named Saul of Tarsus. As they hurled stone after stone at him, Stephen

prayed, "Our Lord Jesus, accept my spirit into your presence." He crumpled to his knees and shouted in a loud voice, "Our Lord, don't hold this sin against them." And then he died.[2]

Stephen's view of Jesus and the glory of heaven made all the difference.

The early church fathers were similarly compelled by the reality of heaven. Polycarp was one of many who were martyred around the year 150AD. He was burned at the stake and was pierced with a spear for refusing to burn incense to the Roman Emperor. On his farewell, he said "I bless you Father for judging me worthy of this hour, so that in the company of the martyrs I may share the cup of Christ."[3]

And we can understand a little more clearly the Apostle Paul's dilemma in his letter to the Philippians:

For to me, living means living for Christ, and dying is even better. But if I live, I can do more fruitful work for Christ. So I really don't know which is better.[4]

Their vision of Christ and his heavenly kingdom affected everything – their perspective, their purpose, their priorities, the people they invested in, and their perseverance.

Their vision of Christ and his heavenly kingdom affected everything

---

[2] Acts 7:54-60 TPT
[3] Fr. Paolo O. Pirlo, SHMI (1997). "St. Polycarp". *My First Book of Saints*. Sons of Holy Mary Immaculate - Quality Catholic Publications. pp. 58–59
[4] Phil 1:21-22 NLT

Remember in the earlier section about the shared table, we spoke of the verse in Jude where he speaks about the 'agalliasis', the extreme joy, of being in his presence when he returns. This joy will eclipse all earthly pleasures and put our tough choices for him and his kingdom in a right perspective.

Now all glory to God, who is able to keep you from falling away and will bring you with great joy into his glorious presence without a single fault.[5]

In fact everyone who is part of the Bride will ultimately be enthralled in heaven with the threefold blessing of

- relationship with Father, Son and Holy Spirit, face to face, unimpeded by our earthly limitations;
- reward that is based on how we have lived our lives on earth. We are not told what this reward will be, but it could be something to do with proximity to the Father[6];
- responsibility in proportion to the way we have used the talents and gifts entrusted to us here on earth.[7]

Steven Covey in his book 'The 7 Habits of Highly Effective People'[8] talks about 'starting with the end in mind'. If there were ever a situation where this was required it would be with the end point of heaven in mind! When was the last time you did a Bible study on heaven, read books on it, made your new year's resolutions or life goals in the light of it, or asked your pastor to do a sermon series on it? What about praying and asking God to renew your heavenly perspective?

---

[5] Jude 1:24 NLT
[6] Matt 20:20-23, Mk 10:35-40
[7] Matt 25:21
[8] The 7 Habits of Highly Effective People, Steven Covey, Simon & Schuster UK

For someone from a very low church background, I surprise myself by having a picture of Jesus in my place of prayer. I find it very helpful, if only because it reminds me that he is real, that one day I will see him face to face. It helps me to imagine his love, his compassion, his courage and his fierce jealousy for my and our love. I was given a copy of the picture of Jesus that was supposedly seen in a vision, and painted by the extraordinary Akiane Kramarik, the child art prodigy, when she was just 8 years old. The picture is called Prince of Peace. It is beautiful.

Interestingly there is another part to this story. Three-year-old Colin Burpo had a near death experience of heaven, in which he saw Jesus, following a burst appendix. It is told in the book and film 'Heaven is for Real'. In the years that followed, his father would often show him representations of Jesus in art, to see if any of them bore a resemblance to the Jesus he had seen in his experience of heaven. The answer was always an emphatic 'no'. One day they were watching a TV piece on Akiane Kramarik. When they showed the picture she had painted of Jesus the Prince of Peace, Colin immediately said, "That's him, that's him". He was very clear that the Jesus of his experience of heaven was the same Jesus she had painted following her vision.

My point is not to prove the veracity of any of these experiences, it is simply to say that we all need a more real, immediate and compelling vision of the Jesus with whom we will spend all eternity, and a longing for the heaven where we will be with him, the new heavens and new earth we have already spoken about. It is a place where righteousness characterises everything , where there is no more death, suffering, crying or pain , a place of incredible beauty, and a place of heavenly reward and fulfilling responsibility.

> *We all need a more real, immediate and compelling vision of the Jesus with whom we will spend all eternity.*

Any bride is naturally consumed with her wedding day, and with her groom. How much is that true of us as the Bride of Christ? Do we need to rekindle our first love, our prayers for and preparation for the wedding day, our heavenly perspective in all we do and in all the decisions we make? I suspect most of us do.

Questions:

- When or where have you most experienced the reality of the person of Jesus?
- How much does heaven shape the way you live now?
- Is there anything you would like to do now to help redress the balance between the heavenly and the earthly in your current priorities and concerns?

Chapter 20

A Heavenly Bridal Charter

I am concluding with a call to action because, as the fabled Greek storyteller Aesop said, 'After all is said and done, there is more said than done.'

How then will we respond to the invitation to be part of this Bride, and to the journey of preparation of becoming the church that Jesus died for and is coming back for?

> '*After all is said and done, there is more said than done.*'

In reality we each have to determine our own response. We are all held to account by Jesus for how we respond to his invitation and challenges. But I thought I'd have a go at putting down my own response. After all we talk a lot about leading by example. But for each of you who have persevered to this point, I'd like to offer you the chance to determine how you want to respond, in the words of the Apostle Peter, to his question, 'What kind of people ought you to be?'[1]

These were my own thoughts for a personal charter for Bridal preparation, in no particular order.

---

[1] 2 Peter 3:11

1. Fan into flame my love for Jesus and pray for his Bride on a daily basis. We get the church we pray for. If it's full of shortcomings, don't criticize, pray!

2. Be patient in loving the church in all its quirkiness, brokenness, failings and stubbornness. It's still the church that Jesus died for, is coming back for, and that he loves passionately. Jesus is building it and I'm not to criticize the job he is making of it. Keep short accounts in all my relationships and be the first to ask for forgiveness.

3. Speak well of the church in general but also of any specific local church that is doing their best with what they have. Honour and support those who serve local churches in leading and in carrying final responsibility. It can be a lonely place.

4. Be part of a local church, making my best contribution (including with my money). Don't ask what my church can do for me, but what can I do for my church. Build radical community where I can, and encourage others to do the same. Stay part of a Missional Community and seek to plant more.

5. Seek to live counter-culturally in every area of life where the prevailing culture is at odds with kingdom culture. Particularly keep individualism at bay by asking in key decisions, "What would be best for my spiritual family?"

6. Stay battle-ready, even in seasons of peace. The enemy is always prowling round like a roaring lion so I can't afford to 'take time out from God'. Resist temptation and keep short accounts over sin, so that the enemy can't take advantage of me.

7. Invest in people by helping them grow as disciples and leaders, so they can go and do the same. Prioritize investing in people who are willing to be multipliers. Seek to make disciples who are committed to practical and supernatural demonstration, and bold proclamation of the gospel of the kingdom.

8. Practice accountability within my local church and in my national role of serving other churches. We all have blind

spots and need to exercise humility. Stay connected to those relationships where I can be honest and vulnerable.

9. Work together with other churches in my city – ultimately we are one body with one purpose. That purpose is to complete the great commission by living out the great commandment and arriving at the great completion, so we can become the beautiful bride that Jesus is coming back for.

10. Live as though Jesus was coming back in my lifetime, preparing for that day in my prayers, lifestyle, priorities and actions.

Questions:

- What would your top ten charter points be? (Try reviewing the chapters and your responses to the questions they have asked.) Write them out somewhere.
- Who will you make yourself accountable to for living by them?

Covid-19 Addendum

It's impossible to finish writing this book during the Covid-19 lockdown without making some comments on the impact both now and in the future of this global pandemic on the shape of the church.

You may remember back in Chapter 16 I made this comment on the massive impact of Disciple-making Movements (DMM) around the developing world: 'I believe that until the church and the world we live in are brought to their knees through persecution, national instability, war, disease or economic collapse, we will not see the same impact' (here in the West). This was written at the start of Jan 2020 before Covid-19 had even been heard of in the UK.

The landscape has been totally transformed by something invisible to the naked eye. A virus. We are currently in our twelfth week of lockdown and counting! Churches have not been able to gather in person, either as congregations or in small groups. Only now can six people get together in open spaces whilst maintaining social distance (2 metres).

Eating round a table has been limited to pre-existing households. Prayer and most other forms of connection have been happening through Zoom, social media or live-streaming. And whilst people are tiring of the social isolation, there is also an underlying anxiety about reconnecting with each other physically because of the risk of what for some may be a killer disease. There is equal if not more anxiety about what the future will hold for employment, personal finances and many businesses. The recession that is inevitable may last for decades, certainly many years.

So all of this has huge impact on how we do church. We don't know how quickly lockdown will end, whether there will be a second spike of the virus, or indeed if this is the first of other perhaps more deadly and contagious viruses to come.

One thing is for sure, scattered church is having its day. Members are caring for each other and their neighbours in local communities. Small groups online are one of the main ways of having meaningful connection for personal support and prayer. Online services are reaching a whole new segment of our society that has not darkened the door of a physical church building for years. On May 3rd 2020, Tearfund published the results of a survey[1] of over 2000 people showing that 24% of adults had listened to or watched a religious service on line since lockdown, and that the number of people praying has significantly increased. These numbers are hugely significant.

There is no doubt that the insecurities felt during this Covid-19 pandemic are challenging all of our traditional securities – income, employment, health, family, community. I don't believe for a moment that God has sent Covid-19, but I do believe he is using it to shake us out of our false securities and comforts. He is leveraging it to demolish some of the idols we have been worshipping for the last 80 years – individualism, materialism, consumerism, hedonism and general self-obsession. The writer to the Hebrews puts it this way: God is shaking everything that can be shaken so that that which cannot be shaken will remain. And we receive a kingdom that cannot be shaken (my summary).[2]

---

[1]

https://www.tearfund.org/en/media/press_releases/many_br its_look_to_faith_during_lockdown/

[2] Heb 12:26-28

I'm reminded of Jesus words to his disciples concerning the kingdom,

Do not be afraid, little flock, for your Father has chosen gladly to give you the kingdom.[3]

It's often said that 'fear not' or 'don't be afraid' occurs 365 times in the Bible, once for every day of the year. I have to confess I've never counted. But we certainly need to hear that phrase every day as we navigate the Covid and post-Covid terrain. Life may well never be the same again. And how we do church may well never be the same again.

Gatherings may be affected for a long time. Being able to hug again may still be a distant thing. Eating a meal with a crowd of friends in close proximity may be a while away. But we are still the church. We are still the hope of the world.

Mission in our new context will be different. But the uptake for example of Alpha online has been amazing. Spiritual hunger is greater than ever, as people are clearly asking for answers. They are looking for security. They are wondering if there is anything or anyone who is truly dependable. They need to see, hear, experience a message of hope. We have that hope. We are hope-bearers to an increasingly hope-less world

We must find the new ways of being, doing and saying Good News. We can build on the new neighbourliness, the increased desire for community, and the opportunities to bring good news to see a great uptake of the gospel.

I have a dream that as we come out of lockdown, groups of believers all over our villages, towns and cities will respond to the new missional opportunities that will exist. I've tried to

---

[3] Lk 12:32 NASB

capture it with a slogan that would be worthy of Boris Johnson's political machinery during lockdown.

- Bless Your Neighbour
- Build Community
- Bring Good News

You are welcome to adopt it if it helps!

And what of those who come to faith. Will they come to our church buildings, or will they simply want to connect with other believers in their neighbourhood? Time will tell.

Church in the house will never be more important as we come out of lockdown. It always was of vital importance. It fuelled the growth of the church in its most vibrant period, for nearly 300 years from the day of Pentecost, AD30, to the day that Emperor Constantine made Christianity the official religion of the Roman Empire, AD323. From 120 in the upper room to 20 million people, half of the Roman Empire confessing Christ. Could we be on the brink of discovering something the early church had known all along?

Certainly our obsession with the big, the glamorous, the glitzy, the performance-based church experience has been shaken, and we've discovered that the church is actually very good at adapting. And those who already had strong house-based church community groups have probably had a head start.

Even so, we long to gather for our big worship, our best preachers, our physical reconnection as the wider church family. But we also don't want to simply aim for 'going back to normal'. This shaking is intended not only to challenge the idols of our age, but to also reset our church patterns and priorities, to re-shape our culture, to fundamentally realign us with his purpose for his eternal Bride.

I believe this pandemic, if we will understand what the Spirit is trying to do, could be a great step forward in Bridal preparation. It has the potential to help us cut away the worthless, to refocus on the essentials, to become more relevant than ever to the world in which we live. We could be the hope that so many are looking for. We could fill the earth in which we live with radical missionary disciples, gathered in authentic gospel communities, serving, blessing and loving those around us with good news. We could be that step nearer to becoming the church that Jesus died for and is coming back for, the glorious Bride of Christ.

Other Books by Nic Harding

- Manifesto, A Blueprint for Missional Church. River Publishing, 2012
- Living on the Frontline, a Beginner's Guide to Spiritual Warfare, republished by Create Space Independent Publishing Platform, 2017
- Reimagine Church, Missio Publishing, 2018.

Further information

Thank you for reading this book. If you would like to know more about Nic's ministry, feel free to contact him at admin@kairosconnexion.org

Nic's main areas of ministry can be viewed on the websites of:
Together for the Harvest (TFH) www.tfh.org.uk
Kairos Connexion (Kx) www.kairosconnexion.org

Nic's church which he originally planted in 1991, and in which he is still based (though not leading) is Frontline Church www.frontline.org.uk